MANAGING URBAN EXPANSION IN MONGOLIA

Managing Urban Expansion in Mongolia

Best Practices in Scenario-Based Urban Planning

Takuya Kamata
James Reichert
Tumentsogt Tsevegmid
Yoonhee Kim
Brett Sedgewick

THE WORLD BANK
Washington, D.C.

ISBN: 978-0-8213-8314-8
eISBN: 978-0-8213-8315-5
DOI: 10.1596/978-0-8213-8314-8

Library of Congress Cataloging-in-Publication Data
Managing urban expansion in Mongolia : best practices in scenario-based urban planning / Takuya Kamata ... [et al.].
      p. cm.
Includes bibliographical references and index.
ISBN 978-0-8213-8314-8 -- ISBN 978-0-8213-8315-5 (electronic)
1. City planning--Mongolia--Ulaanbaatar. I. Kamata, Takuya. II. World Bank.
HT169.M652M455 2010
307.1'216095173--dc22
                                        2010013121

Cover photos: Takuya Kamata/World Bank (center); Michael Foley, former World Bank staff/consultant and photographer
Cover design: The Word Express, Inc.

Contents

Foreword vii

Preface viii

Acknowledgments ix

Currency, Abbreviations, and Definitions xi

Summary xv
Policy Directions and Scenarios xx
Implications for Planning and Development xxi

CHAPTER 1. Introduction: Background, Scope, and Methods 1
Background 1
Scope and Methods 3

CHAPTER 2. Development Context: Governmental, Socioeconomic,
and Local Profile 5
Government and Administrative Structure in Ger Areas 5
Socioeconomic Profile of Ger Areas 6
Current Status and Development Assumptions of Three Ger Areas 9

CHAPTER 3. Land and Housing 15
Legal, Institutional, and Policy Aspects 15
General Household Characteristics 16
Land and Housing in Ger Areas 17
Implications of Ger Area Housing Development Options 22

CHAPTER 4. Water Supply 25
Status of Current Water Supply in Ger Areas 25
City Center Ger (Naran), 11th Khoroo, Bayangol District 27
Midtier Ger (Bayankhoshuu), 8th Khoroo, Songino Khairkhan District . . . 29
Fringe Ger (Sharhad), 9th Khoroo, Bayanzürkh District 31

CHAPTER 5. Municipal Roads and Public Transportation 33
Current Status of Roads in City Center, Midtier, and Fringe Gers 33
Current Status of Public Transportation 34
Options and Challenges for Service Improvements 36

CHAPTER 6. Solid Waste Management 45
Overview of Current Solid Waste Management in Ger Areas 45
Options for Service Improvements for Solid Waste Management 48
Financial and Economic Implications for Improved Solid Waste Service 53

CHAPTER 7. Heating 59
Current Status of Heating in Ger Areas 59
Options for Service Improvements and Financial Implications 62

CHAPTER 8. Electricity 69
Overview of Current Status of Electricity 69
Current Status of Electricity in Ger Areas 71
Options for Service Improvements in Ger Areas 72
Concluding Remarks. 74

CHAPTER 9. Education and Health Services 75
Current Status of Education and Health Service Provision in Ger Areas 75
Options for Service Improvements and Financial Implications 79

CHAPTER 10. Conclusion 81
Implications for Planning and Development 82

ENDNOTES. 85

APPENDIXES 89
   A. Technical Note on the Analysis of the 2008 Household Socioeconomic Survey 91
   B. City Center Ger Planning Illustrations 92
   C. Ulaanbaatar District Statistics. 94
   D. Distribution and Distances of Water Kiosks. 95
   E. Plan of Water Supply Pilot Project in Dambadarjaa 98

REFERENCES. 99

INDEX. 101

Foreword

Ulaanbaatar (UB) city strives to become a well-developed capital with a vibrant economy, a set of advanced land policies, an approach to good management, a plan for improved housing conditions, a healthy and safe environment, a developed social life, a modern legal framework, a responsive and efficient public administration that enables broad participation of the community and the private sector in civil service, and an attractive tourist destination in Asia.

More than 60 percent of UB's population still live in peri-urban informal settlements, known as ger areas, which lack modern infrastructure services such as piped-in water, sanitation, paved roads, public transportation, and so on. Its social infrastructure (health clinics, schools, and housing and recreation facilities) also needs to be improved. The unplanned growth of ger areas and the unprecedented pace of urbanization bring many challenges, including unemployment, traffic congestion, air pollution, and negative environmental impacts.

The recently updated UB City Master Plan suggested the "Compact City" concept, which envisions a densely populated downtown area with a well-developed public transportation system and improved accessibility to the ger areas. The UB City Master Plan also revealed a need for enormous financing to realize the envisioned plans and ideas.

I have the pleasure of endorsing the findings of the report titled "Managing Urban Expansion in Mongolia: Best Practices in Scenario-Based Urban Planning," which has been developed by the World Bank on the basis of extensive discussions with the UB Governor's Office and with agencies and stakeholders. I truly believe that the options for ger area development in UB outlined in this report will serve as a guiding force for our work with the ger area residents, local communities, external partners, donors, and other stakeholders.

BAT Ch.
General Manager
Governor's Office
Capital City of Ulaanbaatar

Preface

The rapid expansion of Ulaanbaatar, the capital city of Mongolia, is one of the country's most critical development issues. Its population has increased by some 70 percent in the past 20 years and now accounts for 40 percent of the total population of Mongolia. The total administrative area of the city is now 30 times larger than the original built-up areas. Most of the expansion took place in the ger areas: low-income areas where basic infrastructure services are poor or nonexistent.

The government has developed policy directions—in its recent national and local development strategies and master plans—to better manage expansion of the ger areas. However, its practices have been mixed. The ger areas continue to expand today, improvements in urban services are slow, and the local government's capacity to respond to these challenges is still limited.

This report provides an analytical framework to assess the viability of various development scenarios of the city. It offers cost and benefit analyses of the choices and tradeoffs relating to housing and urban services. Policy makers and citizens of the city will be able to see the implications of the policy choices they make today. The report will serve as a vital instrument for broad public policy consultations, which are an integral part of the urban development policy dialogue between Mongolia and the World Bank.

Arshad Sayed
Country Manager for Mongolia
East Asia and Pacific Region
The World Bank

Ede Ijjasz
Sector Manager
Sustainable Development Unit
The World Bank

Acknowledgments

This report is based on information from many sources and has benefited greatly from the input of many contributors and reviewers. The work was undertaken by a core World Bank team led by Takuya Kamata and composed of James Reichert, Tumentsogt Tsevegmid, Yoonhee Kim, and Brett Sedgewick. The following consultants formed part of the larger team by contributing to individual chapters: Namkhainyam Busjav (Heating), Erdenebat Ulziidalai (Electricity), Baasankhuu Manduul (Transportation), Jae-Kyu Coi and Kang-Ki Song (Solid Waste), and Geun Yong Kim and Heon-Joo Park (Land and Housing). The team was supported greatly by the help of Nomuuntugs Tuvaan, Otgonbayar Yadmaa, and Vellet Fernandes. Sunjidmaa Jamba was instrumental in helping introduce the team to key government officials, and Altantsetseg Shiilegmaa provided key information to the team about Mongolia's budget.

Others who have contributed to this report include Mila Freire, Songsu Choi, and Salvador Rivera, who graciously served as internal peer reviewer, as well as David Dollar, Arshad Sayed, Michael Warlters, Rogier J. E. Van Den Brink, Sunjidmaa Jamba, Graeme Eric Hancock, Toyoko Kodama, Christopher Finch, Gailius Draugelis, Yoshine Uchimura, and Victor Vergara, who provided valuable comments, advice, and assistance along the way. John Felton provided editorial support. "Cities Alliance"—a multiple-donor grant facility—provided funding for publication and dissemination.

World Bank management provided valuable guidance and support throughout the process, including David Dollar, Arshad Sayed, Ede Ijjasz, Keshav Varma, and John Roome.

This report was developed with the collaboration and assistance of the Government of Mongolia, the Municipality of Ulaanbaatar (UB), and the many representatives from the utility companies that operate in UB. The unique onsite details contained in the report would not have been possible were it not for the many *khoroo, kheseg,* and community leaders, as well as residents, who volunteered their time to meet repeatedly with the task team. The governors agreed early on to help and continued to provide support throughout the process. The project management unit of the International Development Association–funded Second Ulaanbaatar Urban Services Improvement Project provided valuable support in facilitating these meetings and providing sectoral data. Members of the donor and nongovernmental organization community, from the Asian Development Bank to local nonprofits, were willing to inform and guide the process.

Existing reports provided key data and background information for this report. Of key interest were the various reports surrounding the "Study on City Master Plan and Urban Development Program of Ulaanbaatar City" (2008); the draft "Air Quality and Health Impact Baseline Study"; "Heating in Poor, Peri-Urban Ger Areas of Ulaanbaatar" (2009); "Consolidating the Gains, Managing Booms and Busts, and Moving to Better Service Delivery" (2009); "Rethinking the Delivery of Infrastructure Services in Mongolia" (2007); "Capacity Building in Energy Planning" (2002); "Southern Mongolia Infrastructure Strategy" (2009); "A Review of the Mongolian Primary Mortgage Market" (2007); "Mongolia's Urban Development and Housing Sector Strategy" (2005); "Hygiene and Sanitation Situation Report for Ger Areas, Mongolia" (2006); "Mongolia: Exploring Options for Management Contracting-Out in Water Supply and Sanitation Services for Ger Areas in Ulaanbaatar" (2008); and "Assessment of the Child Money Program and Properties of Its Targeting Methodology" (2006).

Currency, Abbreviations, and Definitions

CURRENCY EQUIVALENTS
(Exchange Rate Effective January 2009)

Currency Unit = Tugrik (Tg, or MNT)

US$1.00 = Tg 1,400

Tg 1 = US$0.000714

ABBREVIATIONS AND DEFINITIONS

ADB	Asian Development Bank
Aimag	province
ALAGaC	Administration of Land Affairs, Geodesy, and Cartography
CES	central energy system
CHP	combined heat and power
CMP	Child Money Program
COWI	consulting group that specializes in engineering, environmental science, and economics
CSC	Customer Service Center
CSD	Centre for Social Development (in Mongolia)
C/V	collection vehicle
Düüreg	district-level administrative division, UB
ERA	Energy Regulatory Authority
ESP	Energy Sector Project
GDP	gross domestic product
ger	portable felt dwelling structure, also known as a yurt
ger area	UB exurbs, containing both gers and detached houses
GHG	greenhouse gas
GoM	Government of Mongolia
GTZ	Gesellschaft für Technische Zusammenarbeit
hashaa	land plot

HH	household
HIES	Household Socioeconomic Survey
HOB	heat-only boiler
IDA	International Development Association
IMF	International Monetary Fund
ITS	indoor transformer stations
JICA	Japan International Cooperation Agency
kheseg	microdistrict-level administrative division, UB
khoroo	subdistrict-level administrative division, UB
LD	loading
MCUD	Ministry of Roads, Transport, Construction, and Urban Development
MDG	Millennium Development Goals
MNT	Mongolian Tugrik
MoH	Ministry of Health
MUB	Municipality of Ulaanbaatar
NGO	nongovernmental organization
NSO	National Statistics Office of Mongolia
O&M	operations and maintenance
OTS	outdoor transformer stations
PHC	primary health care
PIR	price to income ratio
PIU	Project Implementing Unit
PMU	Project Management Unit
PPIAF	Public-Private Infrastructure Advisory Facility
PSR	present serviceability rating
RT	return
STF	Small Transfer Station
sum	county-level administrative division, outside UB
TA	technical assistance
Tg	Tugrik, currency of Mongolia
TR	transfer
Tuk	waste collection and transportation company
UB	Ulaanbaatar, Mongolia
UBEDN	Ulaanbaatar Electricity Distribution Network Company
UL	unloading

UNICEF	United Nations Children's Fund
USIP2	Second Ulaanbaatar Services Improvement Project
USIP2 PMU	Second Ulaanbaatar Service Improvement Project, Project Management Unit of Ulaanbaatar City
USUG	Water Supply and Sewage Authority Co. of Ulaanbaatar City
VAT	value added tax
WHO	World Health Organization
WWTP	wastewater treatment plant
XLPE	rubber-insulated aerial conductors
zud	severe winter
State Great Khural	Parliament of Mongolia

Summary

The sustainable development of ger areas in Ulaanbaatar (UB), the capital city of Mongolia, is one of the critical development issues facing the country. The transition to a market economy and a series of severe winters (called *zud*) have resulted in the large-scale migration of low-income families into the ger areas of UB. The city represents 40 percent of the nation's population and generates more than 60 percent of Mongolia's gross domestic product (GDP).

This migration pattern has led to an unprecedented expansion of the ger areas. The traditional built-up areas of the city center comprise some 130 km², but the total administrative area of UB, including ger areas, is now estimated at about 4,700 km². The population of the ger areas is now estimated to make up about 60 percent of the total population of UB. The city's population has grown from 600,000 in 1989 to more than 1 million in 2007 and is expected to reach 1.3 million in 2015.

Basic services are very limited or even nonexistent in ger areas. Nearly 85 percent of ger residents use wood- or coal-burning stoves for heating, in contrast to apartment buildings, which are connected to the central heating system. Ger residents must purchase water at public water kiosks, while apartment residents enjoy reliable supplies of piped-in drinking and hot water. The low density of ger areas, coupled with the extremely cold climate, makes the provision of these basic public services very costly. Poor urban services have also led to environment degradation, including the pollution of air and soil, which poses health risks such as respiratory diseases and hepatitis.

Clearer policy directions, such as the "Compact City" concept of the UB Master Plan 2030, have emerged in recent years to control spatial expansion and promote high-density development for the ger areas. However, the government's practices have been inconsistent. These practices are, in part, a result of limited awareness and understanding by the general public, as well as by policy makers, of the public costs of their actions on land management. Also, many supporting mechanisms, including land valuation and taxation, have not yet been properly developed.

This economic sector work by the World Bank aims to help policy makers and citizens of UB better understand the consequences of their practices. The report provides information for use in public consultation with stakeholders, which constitutes the core of the policy dialogue exercise.

The intent of this report is to clarify the costs and benefits of different development paths. These paths include (a) conversion of ger areas into apartment building complexes, (b) gradual improvement of urban services for existing ger areas, and (c) further expansion of ger areas at the fringe of the city.

Three ger areas were chosen for review as proxies of these paths. A khoroo (subdistrict) in Naran ger represents the first path (the "City Center" ger); another khoroo in the Bayankhoshuu ger represents the second (the "Midtier" ger); and a third khoroo in Sharhad ger (the "Fringe" ger) is the proxy for the last. Cost analyses—as well as some benefit analyses where possible and appropriate—were made for housing and land, water supply, municipal roads and public transportation, heating, electricity, solid waste management, and other social services such as health and education.

Land and Housing: Private ownership of land and houses is generally high. In older and established ger areas, nearly 99 percent of families own their own dwellings and land. The ownership rate is lower (about 80 percent) in newer fringe ger areas where many new immigrants rent their land or houses. Private ownership of land is around 60 percent for apartments and 92 percent for single-family housing.

The size of *hashaas* (land plots) is fairly uniform at about 470 m²–590 m² in all ger areas because residents occupy as much land as laws allow. The average house is slightly larger in the City Center ger at 77 m², compared to 55 m² in the Midtier and Fringe gers. Apartments on average are 37 m², smaller than houses. In the City Center (Naran) and Fringe (Sharhad) ger areas, almost one-half of households still live in gers, while in the Midtier (Bayankhoshuu) ger area, 70 percent live in detached houses.

Apartments are the most valuable assets for households in the city, with market prices on average Tg 43.4 million–Tg 60.2 million (US$31,000–US$43,000). Houses in central ger areas are significantly more valuable, at an average of Tg 29.4 million (US$21,000) than houses in the Midtier and Fringe gers, which cost an average of around Tg 18.9 million (US$13,500) and Tg 17.5 million (US$12,500), respectively. The value of gers is much lower than either apartments or houses: Tg 1,820,000 (US$1,300) in central areas, and Tg 980,000 (US$700) in fringe ger areas.

The mortgage market is still emerging in Mongolia, with only 10 percent of home owners using mortgage loans. Fewer than 20 percent of apartment residents use mortgages. A majority of residents in the three ger areas will not be able to afford to live in any of the apartment buildings that the government proposes to build. Given this affordability issue, alternatives such as low-cost housing and/or low-income public rental housing should further be examined.

Residents in established ger areas are not only more likely to own their homes than residents of apartments, they are somewhat more likely to be satisfied with their homes. In a survey, almost 90 percent of residents in the Midtier ger said they are either "very satisfied" or "moderately satisfied" with their living conditions, compared to 70 percent of City Center ger residents and 80 percent of apartment residents. However, half of residents in the Fringe ger said they are "very dissatisfied" with their housing, compared to only 6–7 percent of residents in other ger areas. The likely reason is that Fringe ger residents are new to UB, and urban services there are the poorest among all ger areas. In terms of the type of apartment developments, most residents would prefer to live in small groups of low-rise apartment buildings rather than in large high-rise apartment complexes.

Water Supply and Sewerage: Residents in all ger areas receive their water through some 500 public water kiosks. Most ger residents say they are relatively content with the current system of water distribution, in contrast to their views of other services and infrastructure such as solid waste collection, local pathways, and drainage. Affordability of water purchased at kiosks is not a major issue either, because the cost is low and residents consume an average of only 10 liters per day per person. Unit costs of water supply and sewerage services are by far the lowest for residences converted to apartments, estimated at about Tg 280 (US$0.19) per m³.

For ger areas, the existing system of public kiosks seems to be the most practical way to provide water. It would be exorbitantly expensive to connect detached houses in established ger areas to the central water supply systems; estimated connection costs range from Tg 5.6 million–Tg 16.1 million (US$4,000–US$11,500) per household, depending on topography, proximity to existing networks, and requirements for wastewater treatment.

Development of kiosks in fringe ger areas should be minimized, however, because of the possibility for relocation of residents, and kiosk water supply is very expensive to develop. The pricing and subsidy of kiosk water supply is a major policy deficiency: the current kiosk tariff of Tg 1,000 (US$0.67) per m³ covers only a fraction of the total unit cost of kiosk water supply. There is no space for cross-subsidization, either. Currently, water is supplied by trucks to about one-half of all kiosks; the rest are connected to networks via water pipes. Converting the truck-supplied kiosks to networked kiosks would make sense only if a drastic increase in consumption is expected, because networked kiosks are only marginally less costly (estimated at about Tg 3,280–Tg 4,260 per cubic meter, or US$2.19–US$2.84) than truck-supplied kiosks (Tg 4,250–Tg 4,260, or US$2.83–US$2.84). Limited capacity in water source and treatment, and the limited sewerage system, would be major constraints for increased demand in the future.

Municipal Roads and Public Transportation: The poor condition of unplanned and unstructured earthen roads in ger areas is one of the most serious concerns expressed by ger residents. Many parts of these roads are impassable for vehicles, have drainage problems, pose traffic safety hazards, and are the source of a substantial amount of dust. Also, the lack of street lights contributes to higher crime rates after dark.

Poor access to public transportation places ger residents at a disadvantage because of their long commuting times to work and schools. Residents in fringe gers tend to rely heavily on public buses because they cannot afford private vehicles. Residents of both Midtier and Fringe ger areas must walk long distances from public transportation drop-off points along major corridors because buses, mini-buses, and taxis cannot or will not operate on the narrow earthen roads in ger areas.

The cost of road improvements for a couple of kilometers within the community to allow minibus operations is similar for each of the three types of ger areas. Typical costs are between Tg 238 million and Tg 322 million (US$170,000–US$230,000) for initial construction, between Tg 1,120,000 and Tg 1,750,000 (US$800–US$1,250) for annual maintenance, and Tg 1,120,000–Tg 1,960,000 (US$800–US$1,400) for the operation of street lights. Per capita, the capital costs would be around Tg 21,600–Tg 40,700 (US$15.43–US$29.07), while maintenance would be around Tg 90–Tg 465 (US$0.06–US$0.33) annually. Road improvement is largely a fiscal capacity issue for the Municipality of Ulaanbaatar (MUB) regardless of the characteristics or location of gers. Financial sustainability of public transportation is another policy issue, because many passengers do not pay fares and the public bus companies face financial deficits.

Solid Waste Management: Ger residents cite solid waste management as one of the worst public services. Solid waste is collected solely by vehicles, the service is unreliable, and collections are infrequent: once each month or even once every three months. Operational efficiency also is very low, with each vehicle collecting from an average of only 100 households per day in summer and even fewer during the winter (seasonal variation of waste quantity is significant: an average per household of 0.9–1.0 kg in winter and 0.2–0.3 kg in summer).

Conversion of gers to apartment complexes in central ger areas would make solid waste collection services more efficient and cost-effective. In areas where gers are not converted to apartments, alternatives such as using a combination of local sanitation workers, collection stations, and vehicles would be much more cost-effective than the current system. Also, waste collection is less costly in the more densely populated ger areas than in spread-out ones.

Capital costs for a system of collection by sanitation workers are estimated at Tg 13.2 million–Tg 19.6 million (US$9,400–US$14,000) for equipment purchases. Operations and maintenance (O&M) costs would be Tg 16.8 million–Tg 35 million (US$12,000–US$25,000) in the Midtier and Fringe gers respectively, depending on density and spatial characteristics. Improvements using the current vehicle collection system would be more expensive, with capital costs of Tg 77 million–Tg 152 million (US$54,000–US$109,000) and O&M of Tg 16.8 million–Tg 59 million (US$12,000–US$42,000) per year. However, MUB objects to the use of sanitation workers for unknown reasons.

On a per capita basis, estimated capital costs range from as little as Tg 1,654 (US$1.18) for the combined approach to as much as Tg 13,658 (US$9.76) for improving the current system. Tariffs vary across districts, at Tg 1,500–Tg 3,000 (US$1.07–US$2.14) per month for each household, with a very low tariff collection rate of 30 percent. While operational and financial details of the *Tuk* (collection companies) are subject to further review, solid waste collection services seem to be a heavy fiscal burden on district governments. Also, MUB would need to develop another landfill soon—at an estimated cost of Tg 51.8 billion (US$37 million)—if current services are significantly improved.

Heating: There are four types of existing heating systems in UB: (a) centralized (or district) heating system, (b) small heating systems for groups of buildings (heat-only boilers or boiler houses), (c) individual heating systems (water heaters), and (d) household stoves. The fuel for all these heating options is indigenous coal or lignite. The use of raw coal in heat-only boilers and household stoves is considered one of the main reasons for the worsening air quality in UB. Other problems include the high cost of individual connections, low heat density, the high rate of heat loss because of the lack of insulation in gers and houses, the lack of heating capacity in the Ulaanbaatar district heating network, and the unplanned and temporary location of *hashaas* (land plots).

Possible options for heating improvements may include (a) connecting more residences to district heating services, (b) creation of small heating systems for groups of buildings, (c) improving the efficiency of household stoves to reduce air pollution, and (d) reducing the use of raw coal for heat-only boilers and individual stoves, and using cleaner fuels instead.

The cost of connecting small businesses and individual households to district heating may vary between Tg 2.8 million and Tg 5.6 million (US$2,000–US$4,000). In some cases, because of low heat density or dispersed locations, the per-unit costs could be as much as Tg 11.2 million (US$8,000). The connection cost in apartment buildings may vary between Tg 560,000 and Tg 700,000 (US$400–US$500) per apartment unit. Connecting individual gers to the district heating system is not considered cost-effective, however. One reason is that the heat load density for individual connections in ger areas is about 40–50 times lower than for apartment buildings. In addition, individual connections would not be economically feasible without proper heat insulation measures. The average ger loses 4–5 times more heat than national insulation standards; individual houses lose twice the national standards.

Heat tariffs need to be reformed significantly because current tariffs do not cover the full costs. Pricing also is regressive, with wealthier households connected to district heating paying for their heating on the basis of space size (rather than actual usage as measured by a meter), whereas ger area residents pay the market price for coal and firewood and get a fraction of the heating compared to apartment dwellers. Overall, lower-income families spend up to 40 percent of total household income on heating.

Electricity: Electricity supply in ger areas is subject to several major problems, including voltage drops due to capacity shortages, insufficient capacity of transformers and substations, and a small number of households without electricity. Most households in the three ger areas under review have electricity, except about 120 families newly migrated from rural areas. Ger area residents who have connections use, on average, about 100–110 kWh of electricity per month and pay about 4–5 percent of their monthly income for it, which is within the internationally recognized affordability limit. Improving service for existing consumers, such as increased capacity at nearby substations and improved metering and wiring, would cost between Tg 280,000 and Tg 560,000 (US$200–US$400) per household.

The cost of new connections for households in the selected ger areas varies between Tg 840,000 and Tg 1,120,000 (US$600–US$800) per connection depending on (among many variables) topography and distance from and available capacity of nearby transformers and substations of the Ulaanbaatar Electrical Distribution Network (UBEDN). Households that currently do not have electricity would not be able to afford new connections. Even though the Energy Regulatory Authority (ERA) has introduced lifeline tariffs for low-income households, very few households have subscribed for these tariffs because either they have recently migrated to the area and have not yet registered or they have not paid their bills for electricity. The lack of proper planning and enforcement among district and municipal authorities also makes it more difficult to provide new connections.

Social Services—Education: Schools in ger areas lack facilities to absorb the increasing number of students. The burden on existing schools can be eased by expanding them or providing additional primary and secondary schools. Either of these actions would require not only investing in facilities but also adding teachers and other supporting infrastructure such as roads, water supplies, and sanitation. The initial cost assessment suggests about Tg 1.8 million (US$1,300) per capita would be needed to provide school facilities on a normal single shift and the supporting infrastructure, excluding remuneration for schoolteachers. Given that expansion of schools is not expected in the short term, providing youth and recreational centers should be considered for prevention of juvenile delinquency. The annual capital cost of such centers is estimated to be around Tg 175,000 (US$125) per child, and costs are Tg 18,200–Tg 25,200 (US$13–US$18) per child for operation. Schools also could be made more accessible to students by improving general road conditions and increasing the frequency of the public/minibuses that many students use.

Social Services—Health: Expanding or adding primary care providers is critical in the remote ger areas that are served by only a limited number of hospitals. Replacing outdated equipment and ensuring deployment of enough staff would prevent the existing problem of underutilization of the facilities: currently not many people use the facilities. The cost of building new primary health care facilities is estimated at Tg 505,400 (US$361) per capita, not including salaries and other variable costs.

POLICY DIRECTIONS AND SCENARIOS

The following policy directions and scenarios have emerged as a result of the above analyses.

Smart growth is critical: It makes economic sense to adopt "smart growth" policies as principal directions in the long run, for example, to increase density in the city center where appropriate while controlling further expansion at the outskirts of the city. In general, high-density development would make it easier to provide better urban services with higher efficiency and lower cost. The public also has the desire to live in high-density development: low-rise apartments or collective housing with utility services. Realistically, however, the majority of ger areas will remain in their current conditions because achieving higher-density development is very complicated, as elaborated below.

Conversion of central gers to apartments will take time: Converting center ger areas into apartment complexes has not progressed as fast as the government had envisaged. One reason is that most ger area residents cannot afford the cost of apartments in the city center. The lack of mortgage finance also makes buying large assets (such as apartments) difficult for many people. A third reason is that the absence of a functioning real estate market—including proper methods for determining prices for private land transactions—has impeded the development of new housing.

Retrofitting urban services in midtier gers is exorbitantly expensive: A majority of ger areas outside the city center are older establishments. Many residents have lived there for a long time and have invested in their dwellings, a large number of which are detached houses. Those residents are relatively content with their neighborhoods and would like to see improved urban services for their houses or the development of low-rise, small-scale apartment complexes. The areas are not suitable for conversion to large high-rise apartment complexes—at least for the midterm—mainly because they are not near network infrastructure except along the major transportation corridors.

Although a minimum level of urban services has reached most of those areas, upgrading services to the full-fledged level now available for apartment buildings would be exorbitantly expensive and almost impossible. The unit costs of services to individual houses are several times higher than for apartment units. Instead, improvements in housing—such as conversion to low-rise, smaller collective dwellings, which might make connection to network infrastructure feasible—could be envisaged if residents' income increases. In the meantime, gradually improving services within the affordability limit of residents and public financial resources would seem the most practical approach for the majority of ger areas.

Room is needed for relocating Fringe ger residents: The situation in the more remote Fringe areas of the city is slightly different. Gers in those areas are inhabited by recent migrants. Their income level is even lower than those of city center residents or the residents of long-established gers. They are farther away from the economic activities of the city and have little access to health and education services. Utility services also are even worse than for residents in established ger areas. Therefore, residents of the fringe gers are very dissatisfied with their living conditions and are ready to relocate, if affordable better housing is available elsewhere. But again, affordability is a very serious issue for the residents because of their economic circumstances.

IMPLICATIONS FOR PLANNING AND DEVELOPMENT

Given the situation summarized above, seven priority areas require attention by the government:

1. Access roads within ger areas: The majority of the residents in ger areas are lower-income and are further disadvantaged by very poor access to markets, workplaces, and education and other services. Modest improvements in the secondary access roads from major corridors to inside the khoroos (including basic drainage and street lighting) would give residents major benefits, including easier access by taxis or minibuses and reduced dust, stormwater torrents, and crime. Therefore, it would make sense to initiate planning for development of access roads within the khoroos. Community-driven initiatives on land re-plotting, if appropriate, would also make it easier to plan roads and provide access for utilities.

2. Better heating systems to improve efficiency and reduce air pollution: Because the development of apartment complexes is likely to take a long time and most ger areas will not be connected to central heating systems in the near future, short-term measures are needed to improve air quality in the city. Such measures could include better access to cleaner and more efficient stoves and fuels, as well as programs to increase the energy efficiency of houses.

3. Solid waste management and community infrastructure: Solid waste management is often listed by ger area residents as one of their most serious concerns. The current solid waste collection practices seem to be very inefficient and costly. Other community infrastructure and services, such as pathways, footbridges, and community youth centers, also would be helpful in meeting day-to-day needs of many ger area communities, given the lack of proper site development and the shortage of schools and extracurricular activities in ger areas.

4. Research on affordable collective housing in midtier gers: So far, all apartment developments have been concentrated in the city center and targeted only for higher-income residents. Therefore, the development of apartments has not benefited the majority of ger residents. However, some residents in the older, established midtier ger areas located along major roads seem willing to consolidate their individual plots and develop low-rise collective housing, which would provide easier and less costly access to utility services. Therefore, it would make sense to begin reviewing the feasibility of affordable collective housing development along transportation corridors and utility supply lines in the established midtier areas.

5. Fringe gers: Providing networked utility services in the fringe ger areas is very expensive. Many residents in those areas are very dissatisfied with current living conditions (including the poor quality and availability of public utility services) and might want to find better housing and economic opportunities elsewhere. For those reasons, a major expansion of networked utilities in the Fringe ger areas does not make much economic sense. Instead, services should be provided at the minimum humanitarian level. Because the future of these gers will depend, in part, on the social integration of new migrants, some lessons about social housing in Hong Kong, China, or Singapore might help Mongolia develop clearer policies.

6. Utility capacity expansion and reforms: The more residents who enjoy a higher standard of living, the higher the required capacity will be for utility services. However, most utility services—water supply, heating, and electricity—already have reached capacity limits. As gradual progress is made on housing and utility services, capacity can also be expanded. Because estimated investment requirements are significant and utility services face considerable financial constraints, reforms of pricing and regulations of utility services will be essential prerequisites.

7. Further research in related sectors: The municipal budgetary resources of UB are quite limited, at about Tg 30 billion–Tg 60 billion (US$21 million–US$43 million) per year. Given the slow implementation of pricing reforms, many infrastructure services in UB already receive large implicit subsidies. Furthermore, expansion of key network infrastructure will easily require investments of Tg 30 billion–Tg 50 billion (US$21 million–US$36 million) or more. Other problems noted in this report—including inadequate housing development, the lack of mortgage financing, and problems in the banking sector—create additional challenges for the housing sector. Further research on municipal finance and the banking sector, including mortgage financing, might help the government develop clearer policy directions.

1 Introduction: Background, Scope, and Methods

BACKGROUND

The sustainable development of ger areas in Ulaanbaatar (UB), the capital city of Mongolia, is one of the critical development issues facing the country. The transition to a market economy since the 1990s and a series of severe winters, called *zud*, have resulted in the migration of many low-income families from the countryside into the ger areas of UB. The city grew from some 600,000 people in 1989[1] to over 1.03 million in 2007,[2] representing 39 percent of the nation's population.

The city now generates more than 60 percent of Mongolia's gross domestic product (GDP) and accounts for 50 percent of the total investment in the country. Given the lack of employment opportunities in other major *aimag* cities, migration to UB is expected to continue. The latest forecasts indicate that the population of UB is likely to reach 1.3 million in 2015 and about 1.7 million in 2025.[3]

The growth has led to an unprecedented expansion of the ger areas. The total administrative area of the city is now estimated at about 4,700 km², which is more than 35 times larger than the original center of the city (around 130 km²). The population of the ger areas is now estimated to make up about 60 percent[4] of the total population of UB.

Basic services are very limited or nonexistent in ger areas. Nearly 85 percent of ger residents use wood- or coal-burning stoves for heating, while apartments are connected to a central heating system. Ger residents must travel to public kiosks as far as 500 m from their homes to purchase water, which they carry back home in plastic or metal tanks. Residents of apartments, by contrast, enjoy an around-the-clock supply of piped-in drinking water and hot water. Provision of very basic public services in the ger areas is very costly, largely due to the low population density and the extremely cold climate of Mongolia.

The lack of basic urban services in the ger areas has also resulted in environmental degradation, including the pollution of air, water, and other natural resources. This situation also poses serious health risks to residents, including respiratory diseases and hepatitis.

Clearer policy directions have emerged to control spatial expansion and to promote high-density development. The "MDG-based Comprehensive National Development Strategy," adopted by the Parliament in 2007, recommended that spatial expansion in UB should be controlled. The "2008 UB City Urban Development Master Plan," which was developed with assistance from the Japanese government, advocated a "Compact City" concept through the more efficient use of land. Implementing this guidance, bilateral donors have offered technical assis-

BOX 1.1.   Ger Areas and Gers

(Photo by Brett Sedgewick, World Bank)

The peri-urban ger areas surround the built-up "downtown" of Ulaanbaatar (UB) city, and are characterized by low-density scattered arrays of fenced property containing informal housing structures, a mix of gers and detached houses. These areas now take up about more than 90 percent of UB. Migrants typically claim open land, install a fence along the property boundaries, and build a ger or a detached house. As the migrants settle down and save money, they upgrade or build the more expensive detached houses on their land. In UB ger areas, some 61 percent live in houses and 38 percent reside in gers.

(Photo by Brett Sedgewick, World Bank)

Traditional gers are nomadic felt tents with wooden lattice substructures, used by Mongolian nomads for centuries. The ger was an ideal living solution for nomads over many centuries because it is mobile (it can be assembled in half an hour), lightweight (one person can erect a ger), and portable, making it well suited for easy moving. The gers have limited space (on average only one room of ca. 28 m²) and do not meet modern standards of living. Cast iron stoves provide heating and are inefficient because of poor insulation (10–15 cm of felt) and create extremely poor indoor air quality.

tance for the introduction of effective zoning regulations, and the government has been taking on large-scale development of apartment residences for UB.

Although policy directions have become clearer, the government's practices concerning the spatial development of ger areas have been inconsistent. The government's early attempts to control migration to UB by imposing punitive settlement fees were struck down by the country's highest court as unconstitutional. The private land ownership laws enacted in 2002, as well as the subsequent land ownership registration procedures introduced in 2005, provide incentives for households to occupy as large a parcel of land as possible. During the pre-election period in 2008, the private land ownership laws were revised to expand residents' land holding entitlements by 400 percent to 500 percent on average, resulting in a land-seizing frenzy around UB.

These inconsistent actions are, in part, a result of limited awareness and understanding by the general public, as well as by policy makers, of the public costs of their actions. There is high susceptibility to ad hoc behavior that places premiums on short-term private gains over long-term value creation in public goods. Many supporting mechanisms, including land valuation and taxation, have not yet been developed to create incentives for long-term value creation.

Therefore, this economic sector work aims at helping policy makers and citizens of UB improve their understanding of the consequences of their choices of policies and practices. Specifically, it intends to clarify the cost and benefit implications of different development paths, with the goal of contributing to the eventual achievement of the Compact City concept. These paths include (a) conversion of ger areas into developments of apartment buildings, (b) gradual improvement of urban services for existing ger areas, and (c) further expansion of ger areas at the fringe of the city.

SCOPE AND METHODS

Because the economic sector work reflected in this report is intended to be an instrument for further public consultation and dialogue, it uses different scope and methods from those of typical sector reports of the World Bank. This report provides cost benefit implications from the residents' point of view and refers to fiscal implications for the municipal government of UB. It does not provide comprehensive sector overview of those urban services, which are readily available in many sector reports, including the 2007 Bank/Public-Private Infrastructure Advisory Facility (PPIAF) report, "Foundation for Sustainable Development: Rethinking the Delivery of Infrastructure Services in Mongolia."

This report is only the first phase of the exercise. It will be shared with stakeholders through a series of workshops and other public outreach activities. Stakeholders include parliament members, policy makers, and practitioners at the national and the municipal governments, district and khoroo community leaders, ger area residents, professional associations, academia, nongovernmental organizations (NGOs), and donors.

Cost analyses, as well as benefit analyses where possible and appropriate, were made for land and housing, water supply, roads and public transportation, heating, electricity, solid waste management, and other social services. Analyses of water supply and social services mostly relied on data from ongoing, donor-funded projects in ger areas of similar characteristics and other existing sector reviews. Quick field surveys have been carried out for roads and public transportation, heating, electricity, solid waste management, and housing and land.

While onsite sanitation is one of the critical issues for ger residents, it is not included in this report, because credible solutions have not yet been developed. Many ongoing experimental programs are so costly that they are not affordable for ger residents. Recommendations from numerous past studies have been deemed inappropriate because of the cold climate and thus have never been adopted in a sustainable manner.

As proxies of the three paths of development—(a) apartment conversion, (b) service improvement for existing ger, and (c) further development of fringe ger areas—khoroos (subdistricts) in three ger areas were chosen for the analyses. In Natan ger, the 11th khoroo, Bayangol District (the "City Center ger"), is expecting large-scale development of apartment and commercial complexes. In Bayankhoshuu ger, the 8th khoroo, Songino Khairkhan District (the "Midtier ger") is chosen for the analysis of the second path. In the Sharhad ger, the 9th khoroo in Bayanzürkh District (the "Fringe ger") is a new ger at the fringe of the city.

The City Center ger mostly borders existing urban areas and has experienced a gradual conversion into apartment buildings. The area partially accesses the standard level of services provided to gers, and it partially accesses more extensive services through the area's proximity to high-density areas. The Midtier ger is bordered on all sides by other ger areas. Residents in the area receive the standard level of services provided to gers. Residents intend to stay in their plots in the long run, making gradual improvements in their housing and expecting improved urban services. In the Fringe ger, residents are still claiming land. Households, especially the new arrivals, lack the standard level of services currently provided to most ger areas. Further description of these khoroos is included in the next chapter.

The khoroo was chosen as a unit of analysis, because it is the smallest administrative division with paid employees, thus allowing for the intimate study of each area but with access to relevant and reliable data. Typically, each khoroo has 1,800–3,000 households with a population of 7,000–12,000. Because khoroo-level data are collected across the city, there is merit in scaling the costs of infrastructure service provision or estimating public benefits. In addition to location, khoroos were selected on the basis of strong support for this study from khoroo leaders and district governors and on the availability of socioeconomic and service provision data from household (HH) assessments and other World Bank projects, donor projects, and NGO activities.

2 Development Context: Governmental, Socioeconomic, and Local Profile

GOVERNMENT AND ADMINISTRATIVE STRUCTURE IN GER AREAS

Ulaanbaatar (UB) is divided into nine districts, or *düüregs*. Six of the düüregs break up the central urban area of the capital city, fanning out to the ger areas. Each düüreg is divided into subdistricts, or khoroos, of which there are currently 132 in the city. Each khoroo is then further divided in micro-districts, or *khesegs*. ger areas are located in all of the nine districts, usually corresponding to lower levels of administrative boundary, the khoroos.

The breakdown of responsibilities, from the mayor's office to leaders of each kheseg, is fairly straight-forward (see table 2.1). The municipality, led by a mayor who is chosen by elected representatives, sets budget and policy, coordinates the districts, and controls citywide activities (road maintenance, for instance). The düüregs, each led by an elected governor, are the smallest administrative unit with budgets available for service improvements. They are responsible for the assets in the area, infrastructure, and service improvements (road construction, health clinics, and schools, for instance).

Khoroos are the primary level of government interacting with residents. To register as a resident, to vote, or to register a car, residents go to the local khoroo office. Each khoroo represents around

TABLE 2.1. Administrative Breakdown of Ulaanbaatar

GOVERNMENT	DIVISION	QUANTITY	APPROX. POPULATION	RESPONSIBILITY	BUDGET (MILLION Tg)	REPRESENTATION, FREQUENCY OF NEW APPOINTMENT
Capital (Ulaanbaatar)	City	1	1,025,174	Budget allocation, services, maintenance	33,502	Citizen's khural (4 years), which selects the mayor (4 years)
Düüreg	District	9	113,908	Infrastructure, tax collection, services	754	2–4 representatives per düüreg elected to State Great khural (4 years), düüreg governor (4 years)
Khoroo	Sub-district	132	7,766	Registration, census, voting, community outreach	Salaries and office maintenance only	Citizen's khural representative (4 years); khoroo governor selected by community meeting (4 years)
Kheseg	Micro-district	ca. 8–13 per khoroo	ca. 597–970	Registration, community outreach	Part-time stipend	Kheseg leader

Sources: JICA 2009 master plan, local interviews.
Note: ca. = Circa; Tg = Tugrik (Mongolia currency).

1,800–3,000 households and has a local office, often combined with a community center. Khesegs are the smallest administrative unit, containing no more than a few hundred households. Each has a volunteer leader who is given a small stipend and is responsible for helping with registration, outreach, health promotion, and local assistance to the unemployed and disadvantaged.

The municipal budget of UB city is quite constrained, around Tg 30 billion–Tg 60 billion (US$21 million–US$43 million) annually. Since 2003, annual city revenues have significantly exceeded expenditures, with only 84 percent of revenues going into the city budget in 2008.

SOCIOECONOMIC PROFILE OF GER AREAS[1]

The socioeconomic differences between the ger areas and apartment areas are as significant as the physical differences. Ger area households are larger, younger, less educated, poorer, and more reliant on social services than are households in apartment areas (table 2.2).

Demographics

The average size of a ger area household is just above four persons, almost one person larger than in apartment areas. In line with the recent growth of ger areas, a high proportion of residents are migrants. Only 50 percent of ger area respondents were born in the district in which they are living, compared to 60 percent of apartment area respondents. More than 93 percent of those ger area residents who are not born in the district came from outside UB. In ger areas, marriage is a dominant reason for migration (more than 40 percent), followed by employment (19 percent) and education (14 percent).

Employment

Rates of employment in ger areas vary according to the source of the data, but unemployment rates tend to be higher in the ger areas than in apartment areas or other areas outside the capital. The 2008 Household Socioeconomic Survey (HIES) reported that, of working-age[2] ger area residents, only 51 percent had worked during the previous 12 months, compared to 56 percent in the apartment areas and the average national rate of 63.6 percent. The 2007 National Statistics Office (NSO) yearbook did not disaggregate employment by the type of area but did approximately substantiate the national employment rate, at 62.4 percent.

Economic activities in the various areas also showed a contrast. ger area residents perform significantly more manual labor than do residents of apartment areas (figure 2.1). Of those employed in ger areas, 30 percent are engaged in construction or manufacturing, followed by 12 percent in trade (wholesale and retail) and vehicle repair. These economic activities contrast starkly with those in the apartment areas, where the most widely held jobs are in education (12 percent), trade and vehicle repair (11 percent), and public

TABLE 2.2. Demographic Summary of Ger and Apartment Areas

	GER AREAS	APARTMENT AREAS
Male	47.1%	45.8%
Female	53.0%	54.2%
Average number of household members	4.2	3.4
Average age	27.9	30.8

Source: NSO (National Statistics Office of Mongolia) 2008.

FIGURE 2.1. Economic Activity of UB Apartment and Ger Area Residents

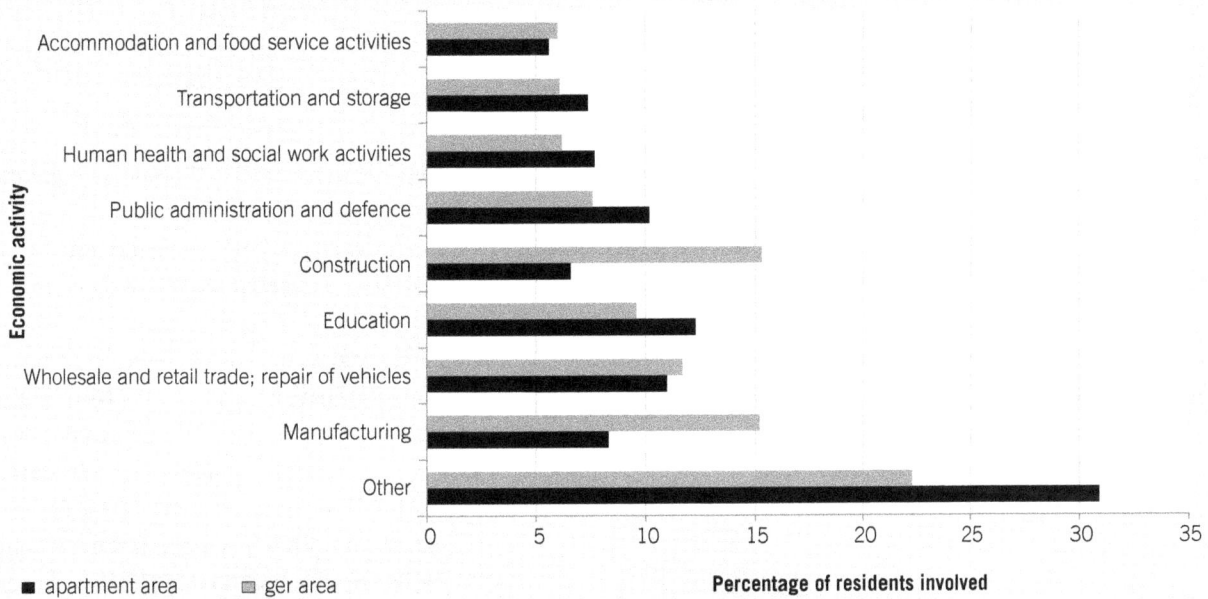

Source: NSO 2008.

administration and defense (10 percent). Also, a higher share of ger residents are engaged in construction work (15 percent) and manufacturing (15 percent), as compared to 6 percent and 8 percent of apartment residents, respectively. These findings suggest that ger residents are more vulnerable to economic downturn than are those in other areas.

Incomes in UB also highlight the differences between the areas (figure 2.2). Ger area median household income (including cash, in-kind, and bonuses) in UB is Tg 2,496,897 (US$1,665). This

FIGURE 2.2. Household Income Distribution, Divided by Quintile

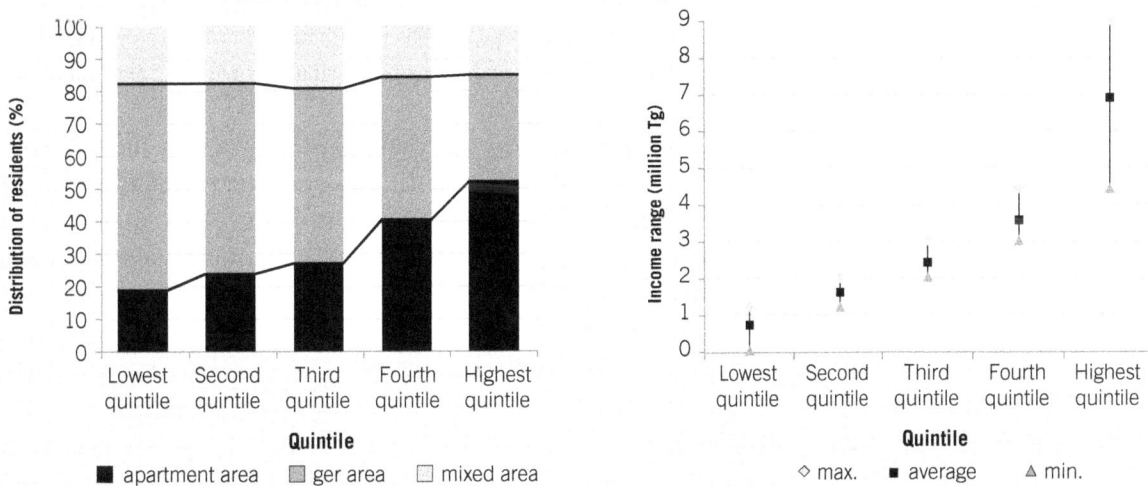

Source: NSO 2008.

income is 43 percent less than for apartment area households. Similarly, income distribution within ger areas and city centers show that even among the highest 20 percent, average income in apartment areas is 17 percent higher than in ger areas.

Benefits and Allowances

Government benefits play a significant role in supplementing the incomes of UB residents, representing 20 percent of ger area income and 14 percent of apartment area income (figure 2.3). These benefits are dominated by child-related payments and pensions; disability payments are also a significant contributor. With the economic crisis, however, these payments are targeted for severe reductions.

FIGURE 2.3. Average Incomes, Including Wages and Benefits

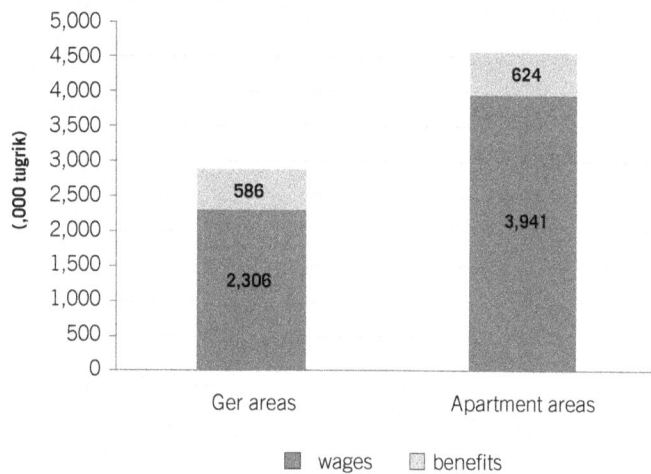

Sources: NSO 2008 and UNICEF 2007.

By far the most common benefit, child-related benefits dominated by the Child Money Program (CMP), are received by 73.5 percent of ger area households. The system is largely universal and multitiered, composed of (a) a Tg 3,000 (US$2.14) monthly payment for every child under 18, (b) a Tg 25,000 (US$17.86) quarterly payment for every child under 18,[3] (c) a new baby allowance of Tg 100,000 (US$71.43) per child; and (d) a maternity benefit of Tg 20,000 (US$14.29) per month for five months during pregnancy and seven months after birth, for mothers below the minimum subsistence level (Tg 30,000, or US$21, in UB).[4] In total, poor families receive Tg 419,333 (about US$280) before the child turns seven months old, followed by Tg 136,000 (about US$91) per year.

State pensions also are significant, providing an average Tg 1.3 million (about US$930) to 30 percent of ger residents. Other benefits received by at least 5 percent of the population include disability payments (average Tg 236,051, or about US$170, received by 7 percent of ger residents), and an "other benefit" that is undefined in the survey (Tg 246,717, or US$176, to 13 percent of ger residents). Several other benefits reach no more than 5 percent of residents.

Until 2007, the CMP had been a targeted, albeit inefficient, social transfer. With the universalization of the CMP and the proliferation of other social transfer programs, these transfers quickly became a substantial part of the Mongolian budget. Three-quarters of the CMP comes from the Mongolia Development Fund, which is mostly financed by mining taxes. With the massive drop in commodity prices in the current economic climate, the Mongolian government is experiencing a corresponding budget shortfall. As part of a budget assistance package financed by the International Monetary Fund (IMF), Asian Development Bank (ADB), World Bank, Japan, and other donors, the Government of Mongolia (GoM) has agreed to propose a major restructuring, with the help of the ADB and World Bank, of its social transfer programs. The government will propose consolidating, reducing, and carefully targeting the transfers to the poor. The goal will be to include only the poorest families, as defined by the National Poverty Line, in the social transfer programs.

PHOTO 2.1.
City Center ger
(Naran)

(Photo by Brett
Sedgewick, World
Bank)

CURRENT STATUS AND DEVELOPMENT ASSUMPTIONS
OF THREE GER AREAS

City Center ger (Naran), 11th khoroo, Bayangol District (Map # IBRD36906)

Naran is one of the oldest existing ger areas, located immediately north of the city. Containing the national TV and radio stations, as well as their antennas, the area is often referred to as the "TV Station ger." The 11th khoroo was originally much larger, but as apartment buildings have been creeping northward and as population has increased, clumps of apartment buildings have broken off into new khoroos. There are plans in the Municipality of Ulaanbaatar (MUB) to build more apartment buildings in the southern half of the khoroo (see appendix B). The khoroo climbs part of the southern slope of one of the many hills in UB, tapering off close to the top of the hill. The long eastern border is one of the main paved roads accessing the northern ger areas and represents the border between Batangol and Chingeltei districts.

In the City Center ger, large-scale development of apartment buildings is expected given the proximity to the city center. The current municipal plans (featured in appendix B) are for permanent structures, most of them 7 to 12 stories, to fill the southern half of the ger area. According to the planning, by 2015 there will be 15,684 households, and the population will reach 65,800 in the development zone (which includes the 9th, 10th, and 11th Khoroos). Facilities will be developed, including schools for 13,160 pupils, kindergartens for 6,580 children, and health clinics with a capacity of 2,300 patients/day, as well as green areas and utilities. Water supply will be centralized, providing an estimated supply of 11,780 m^3/day. Wastewater will also be centralized, using an estimated 2,900 meters of pipes and with collection estimated at 11,780 m^3/day. Approximately 12,500 meters of transmission pipes will provide centralized heating, a load of 63.7 Gcal/hour. Seven substations will supply power to the district, providing capacity of an estimated 32.6MWt. Implementation, including ground engineering, roads, preparatory measures for engineering, gardening and furnishing, will cost approximately Tg 26 billion (US$17.3 million).

PHOTO 2.2. Midtier ger (Bayankhoshuu)

(Photo by Brett Sedgewick, World Bank)

Midtier ger (Bayankhoshuu), 8th khoroo, Songino Khairkhan District (Map # IBRD36904)

The Bayankhoshuu ger lies a few kilometers up the road from the City Center ger's main road, on the other side of a large hill. The main road provides the khoroo's northern border and is the principal source of commerce. This khoroo is relatively flat, with a small lake in the middle that feeds several brick-making enterprises. The lake also effectively collects the solid waste that blows around the neighborhood's streets. The midtier ger areas exemplified by Bayankhoshuu form the mostly continuous mass of the larger ger area. It is surrounded, for several kilometers in every direction, by other khoroos filled with gers. Household plots of land have been oriented along the main road with little planning, thus creating long, uninterrupted blocks sometimes more than 1 km long. The community is entrenched, because residents, having established themselves and their families in the area, are reluctant to leave. Some higher-income residents may wish to obtain private services, such as private water supply connections or private hot-water boilers, for their houses. Other affluent residents might want to consolidate their land plots and build small-scale residential building structures for multiple family dwellings.

Fringe ger (Sharhad), 9th khoroo, Bayanzürkh District (Map # IBRD36905)

Along the northeast edge of UB, the relatively new Sharhad ger area is still expanding, with a comparatively lower density. The khoroo starts in the main UB basin, climbing the edges of foothills. The residents farthest from the center raise livestock for a living; other than this type of pastoralism, urban agriculture is largely unknown in UB. Several bus lines end at the bus terminal just over the nearest border, the only paved section of the khoroo. A largely self-sufficient national mental hospital is also located in the khoroo. The city's main used-car market is located in the neighboring khoroo (17th), providing jobs to many residents. Compared to the midtier ger areas, residents of the far-fringe ger areas are less attached to their land—having only recently arrived in the area—and are, therefore, more willing to move.

PHOTO 2.3. Fringe ger (Sharhad)

(Photo by Brett Sedgewick, World Bank)

MAP 2.1. Ulaanbaatar

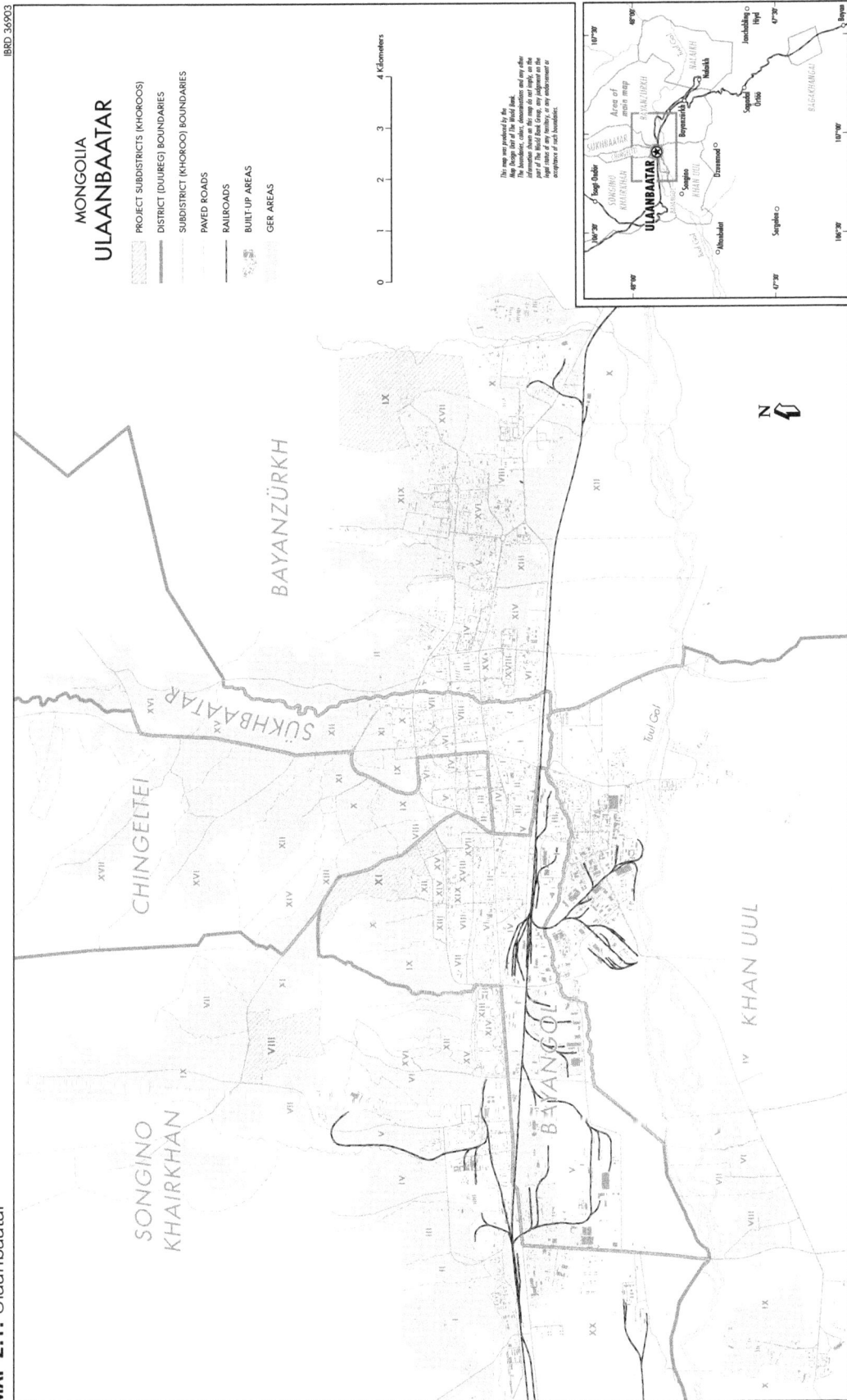

MONGOLIA
ULAANBAATAR

PROJECT SUBDISTRICTS (KHOROOS)
DISTRICT (DUUREG) BOUNDARIES
SUBDISTRICT (KHOROO) BOUNDARIES
PAVED ROADS
RAILROADS
BUILT-UP AREAS
GER AREAS

0   1   2   3   4 Kilometers

IBRD 36903

FEBRUARY 2010

This map was produced by the Map Design Unit of The World Bank. The boundaries, colors, denominations and any other information shown on this map do not imply, on the part of The World Bank Group, any judgment on the legal status of any territory, or any endorsement or acceptance of such boundaries.

MAP 2.2. Bayangol 11th Subdistrict, Naran Ger

IBRD 36906

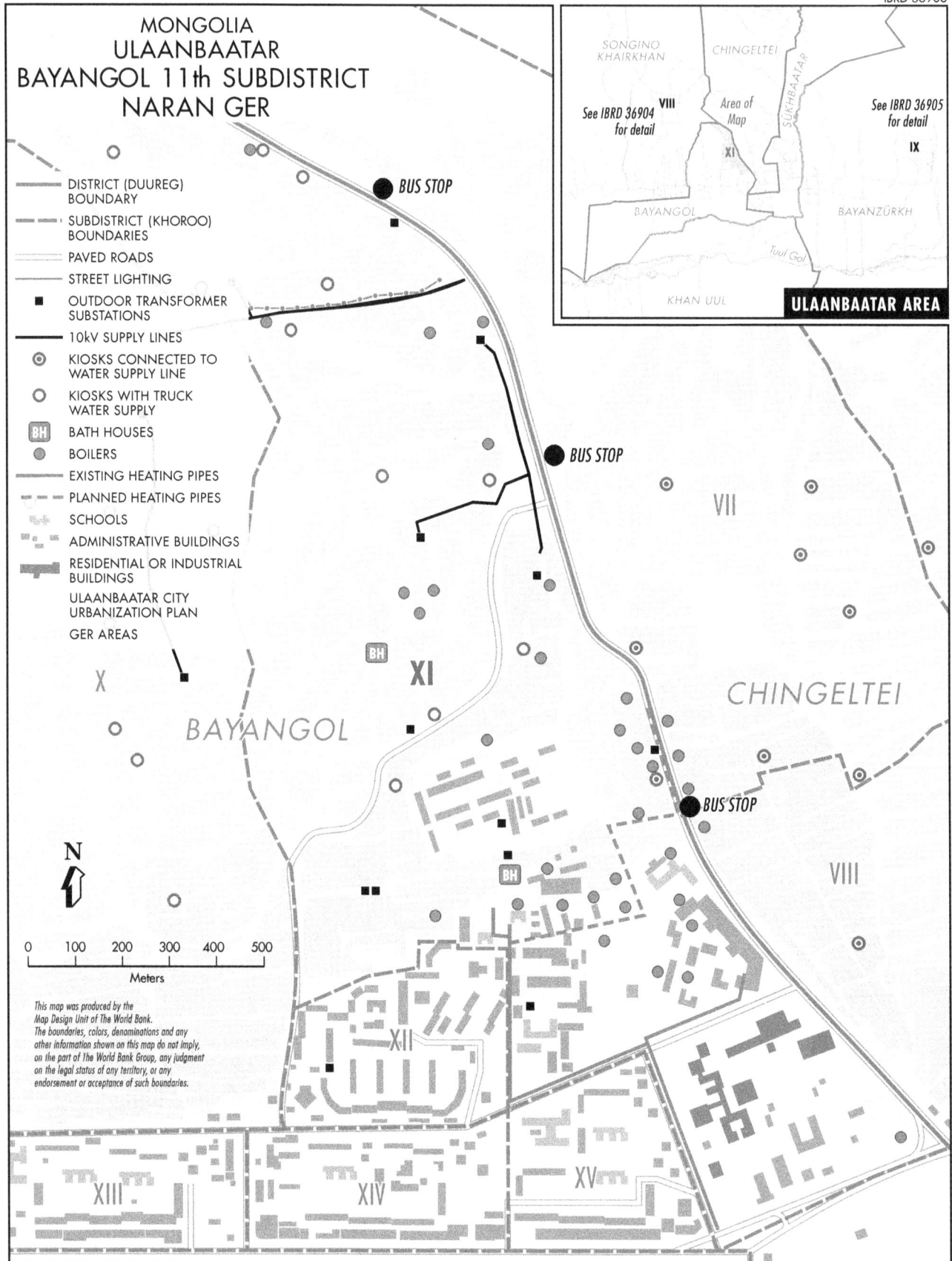

MONGOLIA
ULAANBAATAR
BAYANGOL 11th SUBDISTRICT
NARAN GER

DISTRICT (DUUREG) BOUNDARY

SUBDISTRICT (KHOROO) BOUNDARIES

PAVED ROADS

STREET LIGHTING

■ OUTDOOR TRANSFORMER SUBSTATIONS

10kV SUPPLY LINES

◉ KIOSKS CONNECTED TO WATER SUPPLY LINE

○ KIOSKS WITH TRUCK WATER SUPPLY

BH BATH HOUSES

● BOILERS

EXISTING HEATING PIPES

PLANNED HEATING PIPES

SCHOOLS

ADMINISTRATIVE BUILDINGS

RESIDENTIAL OR INDUSTRIAL BUILDINGS

ULAANBAATAR CITY URBANIZATION PLAN

GER AREAS

SONGINO KHAIRKHAN

CHINGELTEI

See IBRD 36904 for detail VIII

Area of Map

SÜKHBAATAR

See IBRD 36905 for detail

XI

IX

BAYANGOL

BAYANZÜRKH

Tuul Gol

KHAN UUL

ULAANBAATAR AREA

BUS STOP

BUS STOP

VII

BUS STOP

VIII

X

BAYANGOL

XI

CHINGELTEI

BH

N

0 100 200 300 400 500

Meters

This map was produced by the Map Design Unit of The World Bank. The boundaries, colors, denominations and any other information shown on this map do not imply, on the part of The World Bank Group, any judgment on the legal status of any territory, or any endorsement or acceptance of such boundaries.

BH

XII

XIII

XIV

XV

MAP 2.3. Songino Khairkhan 8ᵗʰ Subdistrict, Bayankhoshuu Ger

IBRD 36904

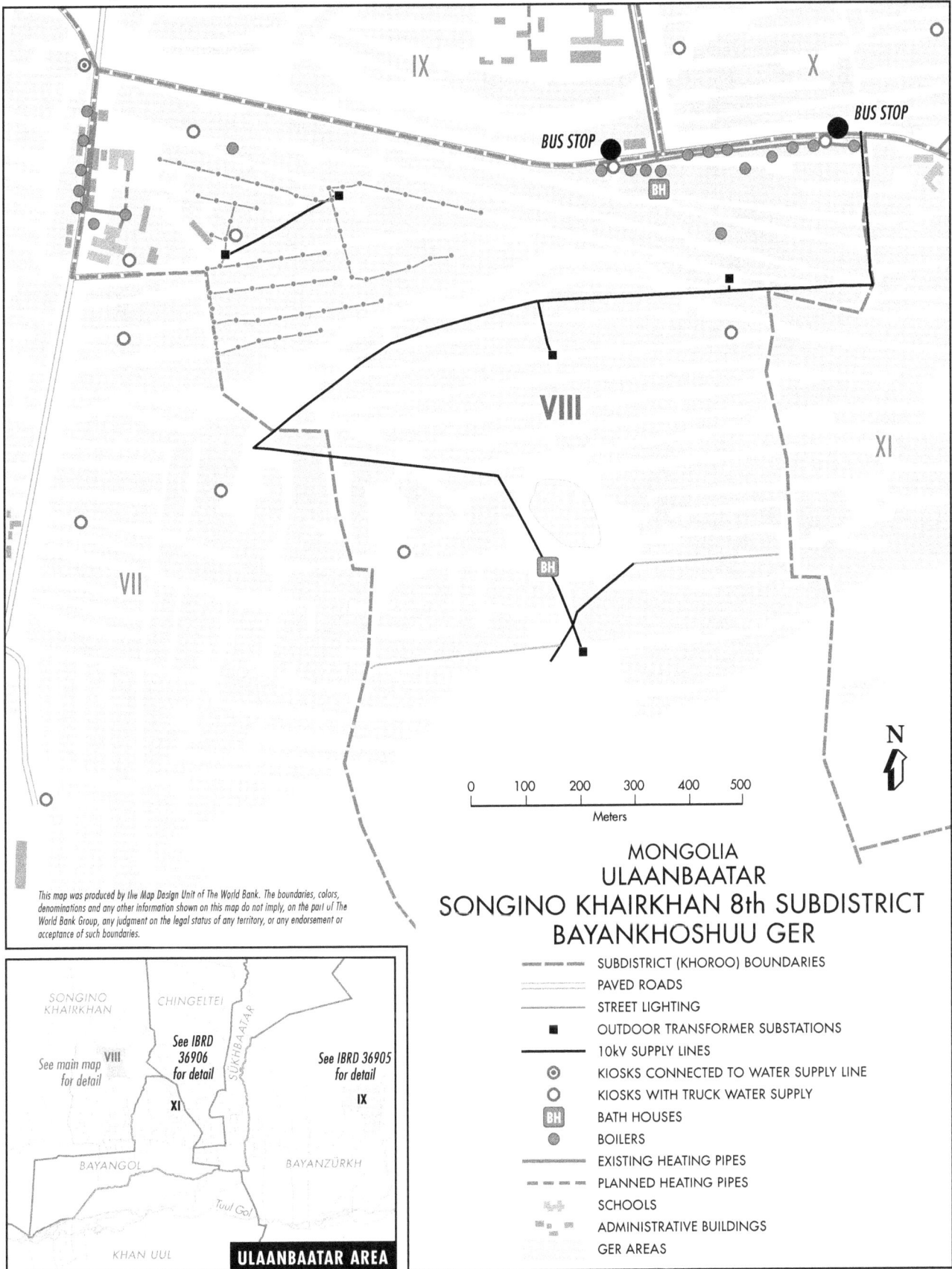

IX

X

BUS STOP

BUS STOP

BH

VIII

XI

VII

BH

N

0   100   200   300   400   500

Meters

MONGOLIA
ULAANBAATAR
SONGINO KHAIRKHAN 8th SUBDISTRICT
BAYANKHOSHUU GER

- - - - SUBDISTRICT (KHOROO) BOUNDARIES
———— PAVED ROADS
———— STREET LIGHTING
■ OUTDOOR TRANSFORMER SUBSTATIONS
——— 10kV SUPPLY LINES
◉ KIOSKS CONNECTED TO WATER SUPPLY LINE
○ KIOSKS WITH TRUCK WATER SUPPLY
BH BATH HOUSES
● BOILERS
——— EXISTING HEATING PIPES
- - - PLANNED HEATING PIPES
SCHOOLS
ADMINISTRATIVE BUILDINGS
GER AREAS

This map was produced by the Map Design Unit of The World Bank. The boundaries, colors, denominations and any other information shown on this map do not imply, on the part of The World Bank Group, any judgment on the legal status of any territory, or any endorsement or acceptance of such boundaries.

SONGINO
KHAIRKHAN

CHINGELTEI

SÜKHBAATAR

See IBRD
36906
for detail

See main map
for detail

VIII

See IBRD 36905
for detail

IX

XI

BAYANGOL

BAYANZÜRKH

Tuul Gol

KHAN UUL

ULAANBAATAR AREA

FEBRUARY 2010

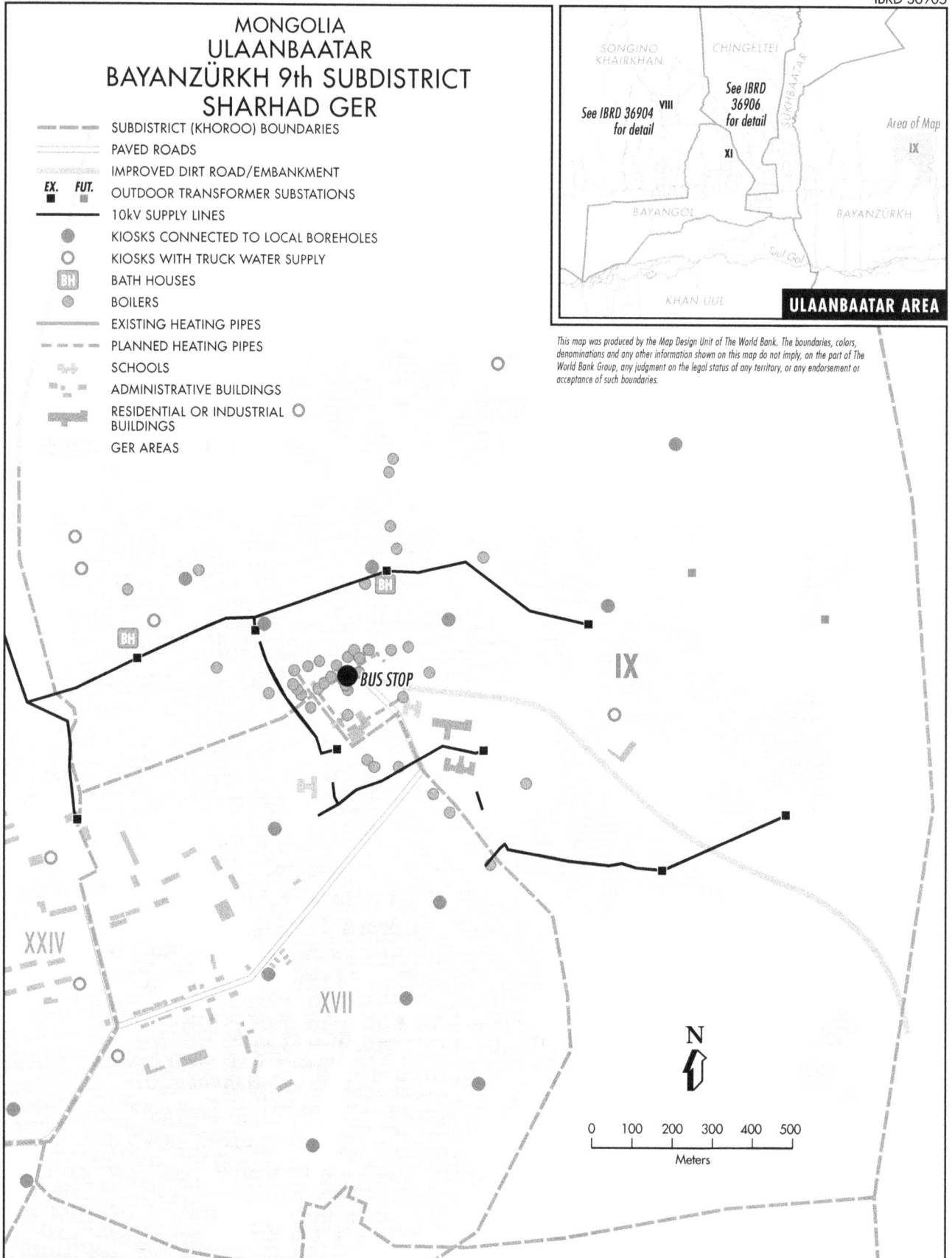

MAP 2.4. Bayanzürkh 9th Subdistrict, Sharhad Ger

IBRD 36905

MONGOLIA
ULAANBAATAR
BAYANZÜRKH 9th SUBDISTRICT
SHARHAD GER

SUBDISTRICT (KHOROO) BOUNDARIES

PAVED ROADS

IMPROVED DIRT ROAD/EMBANKMENT

EX.   FUT.

OUTDOOR TRANSFORMER SUBSTATIONS

10kV SUPPLY LINES

KIOSKS CONNECTED TO LOCAL BOREHOLES

KIOSKS WITH TRUCK WATER SUPPLY

BATH HOUSES

BOILERS

EXISTING HEATING PIPES

PLANNED HEATING PIPES

SCHOOLS

ADMINISTRATIVE BUILDINGS

RESIDENTIAL OR INDUSTRIAL BUILDINGS

GER AREAS

SONGINO KHAIRKHAN

CHINGELTEI

SUKHBAATAR

See IBRD 36904 for detail

VIII

See IBRD 36906 for detail

Area of Map

IX

XI

BAYANGOL

BAYANZÜRKH

Tuul Gol

KHAN UUL

ULAANBAATAR AREA

This map was produced by the Map Design Unit of The World Bank. The boundaries, colors, denominations and any other information shown on this map do not imply, on the part of The World Bank Group, any judgment on the legal status of any territory, or any endorsement or acceptance of such boundaries.

BH

BH

BUS STOP

IX

XXIV

XVII

N

0   100   200   300   400   500

Meters

3 Land and Housing

This chapter is based on a survey that the study team organized in three ger areas and a representative apartment area to assess land ownership, dwelling types, and households' preferences for housing options and affordability issues.[1] The survey analysis intends to highlight issues related to financing and affordability for housing.

LEGAL, INSTITUTIONAL, AND POLICY ASPECTS

Land ownership in Mongolia has gradually been privatized since the country's transition to a market economy in the 1990s. There has been a series of land laws or amendments to existing laws; the current land ownership in Mongolia is based on the 2002 "Law on Allocation of Land to Mongolian Citizens for Ownership." According to this law, the land tenure system in Mongolia is composed of a combination of three land rights: "ownership" only for Mongolian citizens; "possession rights" for up to 60 years, with possible extension, available to Mongolian citizens and joint ventures; and "land use rights," valid up to five years with possible extension, for which foreigners are also eligible.

Land ownership is tied to the land fee system, which the government introduced in 1997 under the "Law of Mongolia on Land Fees." The law stipulates that individuals, business entities, and organizations that own or use land are subject to land fees. For cities, villages, and other settled places, the land fee ranges from 0.1 to 1 percent of the base land value. The land fee is determined by the central government taking into account certain fixed parameters, including location and land use as well as socioeconomic, geological, and environmental conditions.[2] The city of Ulaanbaatar (UB) is divided into five land valuation zones depending on location and income level, and the land fee is applied uniformly to the properties in each zone.

The Government of Mongolia (GoM) has fully privatized ownership of land for "family needs" or residential purposes. The "Law on Allocation of Land to Mongolian Citizens for Ownership" stipulates that each household is entitled to the following for ownership: up to 700 m² in UB; up to 3,500 m² in aimag; or up to 5,000 m² in total. The associated land fee is set low: about 90 percent of the land fee up to 700 m² is exempt.[3] The fees are estimated on an annual basis and charged quarterly; collection is managed at the district government level.

Land management is currently done by the Administration of Land Affairs, Geodesy, and Cartography (ALAGaC), under the Ministry of Construction and Urban Development. The mandate of the ALAGaC is to oversee and implement the government's land policy, to manage and update geodetic and cartographic information and databases, and to improve the cadastral system by carrying out cadastral surveys and establishing a unified database. In addition to the ALAGaC, there are land departments in nine districts of UB that process and manage registration. Those departments are also responsible for mediating any disputes over land ownership, as well as evicting the occupants of illegal settlements.

Although there have been numerous initiatives to improve land management—mostly funded by external donors—the cadastral system (surveys of land boundaries) generally suffers from a lack of administrative capacity and the limited availability of adequate databases. This problem is caused mostly by unsatisfactory or insufficient cadastral surveys and mapping and inadequate registration of land-owners, users, and possessors.

On the legal side, existing cadastral law does not include procedures for property registration. There also is no legal framework for handling disputes arising during cadastral surveys; such disputes are increasingly common in residential areas. Institutional roles and responsibilities at different levels of government are not clearly delineated, and there is a general lack of administrative capacity, especially at the district levels that are mainly responsible for managing land registration. The National Land Information System—a comprehensive cadastral database connecting the collection of data from around the country—was planned for implementation but has experienced some delay.[4]

The GoM launched more recently the 40,000 housing units program around 2003 and the 100,000 housing construction policy around 2008. These are supply-driven housing developments that focus mainly on providing apartments and core supporting infrastructure. However, the effectiveness and viability of these programs remain questionable, as there are still critical systemic deficiencies in housing finance and affordability. In addition, there are no institutional systems to provide low-cost housing for middle- and low-income households, which compose about 70 percent of all households.

GENERAL HOUSEHOLD CHARACTERISTICS

For the surveyed households, the average age of residents ranges from 44.4 to 48.8, and the number of people per household ranges from 3.4 to 4.9 (see table 3.1).

About half of ger residents are reported to be unemployed, consistent with the findings from the Household Socioeconomic Survey (HIES), which showed about 56 percent of the sample in ger areas reported not to have worked during the previous 12 months. The percentage of unemployed is

TABLE 3.1. Survey Respondents' Average Age (years) and Household Size (number of persons)

	AVERAGE AGE OF HH	AVERAGE HH SIZE	RESPONDENTS (%)	
			HEAD OF HH	SPOUSE
City Center ger (Naran)	47.1	4.9	65.1	34.9
Midtier ger (Bayankhoshuu)	48.8	4.3	97.7	2.3
Fringe ger (Sharhad)	44.4	4.5	68.0	32.0
Apartment area	46.0	3.4	76.1	23.9

Source: World Bank Task Team Survey 2009.
Note: HH = Household.

highest in the Midtier and Fringe gers: 62.6 percent and 54.3 percent, respectively, in contrast with 21.1 percent in the apartment area (see table 3.2).

The survey results highlight income and wealth gaps between ger and apartment areas. Average monthly income in the Midtier and Fringe gers is only about 50 percent of apartment areas. The income level in the City Center ger is higher than the Midtier and Fringe gers, at US$223 per month, which is about 70 percent of apartment areas' income. As for assets and liabilities, there is again a stark contrast between ger and apartment residents. Differences are most notable between apartment areas and the Fringe ger, where the total reported assets are only 30 percent of the apartment residents (see table 3.3).

LAND AND HOUSING IN GER AREAS

Similar to most ger areas, dwelling types in the three ger areas consist of a combination of gers and detached houses, and the distribution of different dwelling types reflects the locations of the areas. In the City Center ger, a majority of people (59 percent) still live in gers. This arrangement is because the area is still expanding with people settling in the hilly side of the district. In Bayankhoshuu, the Midtier ger, more than 70 percent of households live in detached houses, consistent with the fact that this ger area was established a relatively long time ago. In the Fringe ger, more than one-half the residences are gers because this is a newly established and still-growing area (see table 3.4).

TABLE 3.2. Employment Status (% frequency)

	WAGE EMPLOYEE	TEMPORARY OR SEASONAL EMPLOYEE	SELF-EMPLOYED (BUSINESS OWNERS, ETC.)	UNEMPLOYED
City Center ger	27 (28.0)	0 (0.0)	39 (21.1)	44 (50.9)
Midtier ger	14 (10.5)	6 (5.3)	22 (21.6)	68 (62.6)
Fringe ger	26 (24.3)	3 (1.5)	21 (19.9)	60 (54.3)
Apartment area	43 (39.4)	10 (9.2)	33 (30.3)	23 (21.1)

Source: World Bank Task Team Survey 2009.
Note: Numbers in parentheses show percentage.

TABLE 3.3. Household Assets, Liability, Monthly Income, and Savings (US$)

	TOTAL ASSETS					
	ILLIQUID ASSETS (PROPERTY)	LIQUID ASSETS (CASH, STOCKS, CARS)	TOTAL	TOTAL LIABILITIES	MONTHLY INCOME	MONTHLY SAVINGS
City Center ger	21,920	4,381	26,196	234	223	70
Midtier ger	13,521	935	14,454	42	154	14
Fringe ger	8,958	312	9,266	46	164	5
Apartment area	26,444	1,362	27,806	2,049	319	21

Source: World Bank Task Team Survey 2009.

TABLE 3.4. Dwelling Types in Three Ger Areas (% of respondents in ger area)

	GER	(%)	DETACHED	(%)	APARTMENT	(%)	TOTAL HHs
City Center ger	1,800	59	1,100	36	150	5	3,050
Midtier ger	460	29	1,151	71	—	—	1,611
Fringe ger (Sharhad)	1,418	58	1,015	42	—	—	2,433

Source: Statistics from district government offices in UB city 2008.
Note: — = Not Applicable.

The average size of land plots in the three areas is less than the 700 m² size of a hashaa, which individual households are entitled to by law. For gers, average land size ranges from 470 m² to 589 m², and the average number of walls in the three gers areas is more or less the same, just under five. For detached houses, plot sizes range from 501 m² to 593 m², with the average number of rooms ranging from 2.3 to 3.5. In the case of detached houses, the closer to the center of Ulaanbaatar that households are located, the larger the average plot size and house (see table 3.5).

Most households in ger areas own their residence and the land attached to it. In case of the Fringe ger, the share of income paid as rent is higher. This fact could be because the residents have a very low income and cannot pay an up-front land registration fee (average Tg 10,000/US$7.14 for migrants; Tg 5,000/US$3.57 for intracity migrants) and hence residents rent gers temporarily (see table 3.6). Another explanation is that people plan to stay in the fringe area for only a short

TABLE 3.5. Size of Land and Houses in Three Ger Areas

	LAND SIZE (m²)	# OF WALLS	LAND SIZE (m²)	HOUSE SIZE (m²)	# OF ROOMS	APT. SIZE (m²)	# OF ROOMS
City Center ger (Naran)	535.7	4.8	593.5	76.5	3.5	59.0	1.9
Midtier ger (Bayankhoshuu)	589.3	4.9	546.8	55.4	2.9	—	—
Fringe ger (Sharhad)	469.2	4.8	501.3	54.0	2.3	—	—
Apartment area	—	—	—	—	—	36.7	2.1

Source: World Bank Task Team Survey 2009.
Note: — = Not Applicable.

TABLE 3.6. Ownership Patterns for Housing and Land (% frequency)

	OWNED	RENT	OTHERS	PRIVATE	STATE-OWNED*	OTHERS-OWNED
City Center ger	108 (97.3)	1 (2.7)	0 (0.0)	109 (99.1)	0 (0.0)	1 (0.9)
Midtier ger	108 (98.8)	2 (1.2)	0 (0.0)	84 (87.9)	23 (6.7)	2 (5.4)
Fringe ger	100 (81.5)	10 (18.5)	0 (0.0)	96 (75.7)	1 (0.5)	12 (21.4)
Apartment area	100 (91.8)	7 (6.4)	2 (1.8)	65 (59.6)	36 (33.0)	8 (7.4)

Source: World Bank Task Team Survey 2009.
Note: *In the case of apartment residents in the City Center ger, about 70 percent responded that their land was state-owned (not privately owned). Following the definition of three types of land ownership, they could have either possession rights or land-use rights. Numbers in parentheses mean percentage.

period of time before moving to a different location. In addition, ger residents reported that they paid about Tg 16,800 (US$12) per year in land fees; those living in detached houses paid about Tg 29,400 (US$21) and apartment residents paid about Tg 211,400 (US$151).

The unit price analysis of existing detached houses and apartments shows that the prices of apartments are about 2.5 to 3 times higher than are those of detached houses (see table 3.7). The prices of detached houses per square meter range from Tg 324,940 to Tg 449,960 (US$232 to US$321), while the apartment unit cost for the City Center ger and apartment areas is Tg 1,076,600 (US$760) and Tg 1,226,960 (US$876), respectively. Apartments in the City Center ger were completed in 2005, and apartment areas include those built during the late 1990s, early 2000s, and, most recently, in 2009 (see table 3.7).

The average price increase for detached houses varies. The highest price increase is seen in detached houses in the City Center ger. Although generalizing price trends based on a small sample size is difficult, the analysis shows that the closer to the city center, the higher the price. The price increase is most evident in the City Center ger area and least in the Fringe ger area. As for the annual costs of operation and maintenance, ger residents reported that they spend Tg 700 to Tg 2,800 (US$0.5 to US$2.0) per m^2, a contrast with the cost for apartments, which ranged from Tg 10,080 to Tg 13,020 (US$7.2 to US$9.3) per m^2. The average price of a ger ranged from Tg 29,400 to Tg 8.5 million (US$21 to US$6,071) with average of Tg 607,600 (US$434).

Housing finance is done mostly through personal savings, and only a small percentage of housing finance is possible through loans from banks or other formal sources. In the case of detached houses, only 2 to 9 percent of the total price is financed through loans. The analysis shows that households in the Midtier ger and the Fringe ger had very limited access to bank loans, amounting to less than 5 percent of the total housing price. Apartment residents, however, reported that they borrowed a higher portion from banks or other creditors: 10.4 percent and 19.3 percent in the City Center ger apartment and apartment areas respectively (see table 3.8). This finding reflects the fact that mortgage lending for housing is still an evolving concept and only the well-to-do can borrow from financial institutions.

TABLE 3.7. Housing Prices and Annual Operation and Maintenance Costs (Tg per m^2)

LOCATION	DWELLING TYPE	ESTIMATED CURRENT PRICE	AVERAGE ANNUAL PRICE INCREASE	ANNUAL O&M COST
City Center ger (Naran)	Ger	—	—	700
	Detached house	434,980	29.0%	7,140
	Apartment	1,076,600	15.5%	13,020
Midtier ger (Bayankhoshuu)	Ger	—	—	140
	Detached house	324,940	24.2%	1,680
Fringe ger (Sharhad)	Ger	—	—	140
	Detached house	449,960	15.7%	2,800
Apartment area	Apartment	1,226,960	NA	10,080

Source: World Bank Task Team Survey 2009.
Note: Operation and maintenance (O&M) costs do not include utilities, only costs incurred by living in the houses.
— = Not Applicable; NA = Not Available.

TABLE 3.8. House Financing Sources (million Tg)

		SELF-FINANCING	(%)	LOANS FROM BANKS OR OTHERS	(%)	TOTAL
City Center ger	Detached houses	7,197	91.2	692	8.8	7,888
	Apartment	31,510	89.6	3,653	10.4	35,162
Midtier ger	Detached houses	10,521	97.7	242	2.2	10,765
Fringe ger	Detached houses	5,487	95.3	267	4.7	5,754
Apartment area		31,245	80.7	7,463	19.3	38,709

Source: World Bank Task Team Survey 2009.

As for satisfaction with housing conditions, there seem to be diverging views among khoroos. Almost all residents in the Midtier ger said they were "very satisfied" or "moderately satisfied" with their housing. In the Fringe ger, however, more than one-half of survey respondents voiced a lack of satisfaction with their housing (see table 3.9). Such a difference is probably caused by the fact that the Midtier ger has existed for a long time and residents have had the time to improve their housing conditions, while Fringe ger residents are relatively newly settled and hence have not had the time and opportunity to improve their situations. In the City Center ger and apartment areas, a majority of residents indicated they were comfortable with their housing. As to the reasons for dissatisfaction with housing, residents in both the City Center ger and the Midtier ger ranked water supply, drainage, and sanitation as the most immediate concerns. Fringe ger residents ranked the size of rooms, lack of a proper kitchen, and heating as reasons for dissatisfaction, in addition to water supply, drainage, and sanitation.

While ger residents expressed a relative comfort in their housing conditions, with the exception of the Fringe ger (Sharhad), survey respondents seem quite dissatisfied with the broader environment in which they live. This dissatisfaction is most apparent in Fringe ger, where more than 90 percent of respondents said they were "very dissatisfied." In contrast, most residents in the Midtier ger answered that they were "moderately" or "very satisfied" with their living environment (see table 3.10). The differences between the Midtier ger and Fringe ger may be attributed to their respective characteristics as ger areas: the Midtier ger has existed for many years, while the Fringe ger is relatively new and still expanding. In the Midtier ger, more than 70 percent of residents live in detached houses, indicating that the population has been there for a long time; this finding also can be linked to the high level of satisfaction with housing conditions.

TABLE 3.9. Level of Satisfaction with Housing Conditions (% of respondents in ger area)

	VERY SATISFIED	MODERATELY SATISFIED	MODERATELY DISSATISFIED	VERY DISSATISFIED
City Center ger	9.8	63.2	20.2	6.8
Midtier ger	46.8	46.7	5.3	1.2
Fringe ger (Sharhad)	4.4	37.3	8.3	50.0
Apartment area	32.1	53.2	9.2	5.5

Source: World Bank Task Team Survey 2009.

TABLE 3.10. Level of Satisfaction with Living Environment (% of respondents in ger area)

	VERY SATISFIED	MODERATELY SATISFIED	MODERATELY DISSATISFIED	VERY DISSATISFIED
City Center ger	6.5	26.9	23.8	42.8
Midtier ger	36.3	38.6	22.8	2.3
Fringe ger	0.0	1.9	7.8	90.3
Apartment area	17.6	27.8	15.7	38.9

Source: World Bank Task Team Survey 2009.

Asked why they are dissatisfied with their living environment, Fringe ger residents pointed to a range of social and public infrastructure deficiencies, including school facilities, health services, roads, public parks, garbage collection, and so forth. For City Center ger and Midtier ger residents, access to school and health services seems to be less of a concern, but road access, limited public space, garbage collection, air pollution, and crime were rated as important reasons for dissatisfaction in their living environment. In the case of apartment area residents, air pollution, limited public space, and traffic congestion were rated as the primary reasons.

Preferred Dwelling Type and Development of Khoroo Areas

In light of the government policy to modernize existing ger areas by building apartment complexes, ger areas in the vicinity of the City Center and Midtier ger areas will develop apartment complexes or a combination of apartments and detached houses. Survey questionnaires included households' preferences for dwelling type and development patterns in khoroo areas to determine how the city government's policy is in line with ger residents' preferences for housing and development options.

The survey analysis shows that a conversion to apartments seems to be the option most preferred among residents, especially in the City Center ger and Fringe ger (see table 3.11). In the Fringe ger, more than 95 percent of residents said they would like the area to be developed with apartment

TABLE 3.11. Preferred Options for Khoroo Development (% frequency)

	CITY CENTER GER	MIDTIER GER	FRINGE GER
Build apartments in all khoroo areas.	61.6	16.4	95.1
Redevelop entire areas of the khoroo with a mix of apartments and detached houses.	21.4	17.5	1.0
Build apartments in some parts of the khoroo.	2.0	17.5	1.5
Develop a mix of apartments and detached houses in some ger areas.	1.3	24.0	0
Do not redevelop the area but improve existing housing and supporting infrastructure.	13.0	24.0	2.4
Keep the khoroo as it is.	0.7	0.6	0

Source: World Bank Task Team Survey 2009.

complexes. Because the same residents are most dissatisfied with their housing and living environment, it may be that the residents see apartments as the ultimate solution for improving those issues. In the City Center ger, more than 60 percent of residents preferred an option to convert their district into an apartment area; a minority favored redevelopment with a combination of apartments and detached houses. About 13 percent of the City Center ger residents responded that they would not like to see the area developed but would prefer to improve existing houses or supporting infrastructure.

Responses from the Midtier ger were somewhat different from the other two khoroos. Residents in the Midtier ger seem to want to maintain the current characteristics of gers with a partial development of their khoroo, including a mix of apartments and detached houses—or keeping the khoroo as it is while improving existing houses and infrastructure. This response is probably explained by the relatively high level of satisfaction with housing conditions and the living environment expressed by these residents.

In general, surveys found that ger residents seem to prefer apartment buildings over single detached houses or gers. As for a particular type of apartments, these residents said they would prefer low-rise rather than high-rise buildings. A large share of residents in the City Center and Midtier gers said they wished to live in apartment buildings of five stories or less, with one or two buildings grouped together in a complex. They chose this style in preference to high-rise buildings (10 stories or more) with multiple buildings grouped together. The focus group interview also suggested that many residents are interested in low-rise, multifamily buildings. In the case of the Fringe ger, where about 95 percent of survey respondents answered that they would like their khoroo to be developed into an apartment area, residents, in fact, said they would prefer to live in newly built detached houses. This response may reflect the residents' awareness that their income level is below what is required for apartment buildings (see table 3.12).

TABLE 3.12. Preferred Dwelling Type (% frequency)

	CITY CENTER GER	MIDTIER GER	FRINGE GER
High-rise apartment buildings	14.9	6.9	37.1
Low-rise apartment buildings	69.3	79.3	0
Newly built detached houses	15.8	13.8	47.4
Others (ger, dormitory, etc.)	0	0	15.5

Source: World Bank Task Team Survey 2009.
Note: High-rise apartment buildings are 10 stories or more with multiple buildings in a complex; low-rise apartment are five stories or less with one or two buildings in one complex.

IMPLICATIONS OF GER AREA HOUSING DEVELOPMENT OPTIONS

Implications for GoM: The earlier survey results suggest the following implications when considering ger housing development options.

❑ Residents of most ger areas seem generally content with their housing. In particular, families who have lived in the area for a long period have replaced gers with detached houses, and they are quite comfortable with their current housing. An exception is found in the remote Fringe ger area, where members of households expressed a very low level of satisfaction; this response reflected the characteristics of that area, which is fairly new and still expanding.

◻ By contrast, ger area residents seem generally dissatisfied with the broader environment in which they live. This response is mainly the result of factors such as air pollution and the lack of key infrastructure and social facilities, including roads, garbage collection, and public space.

◻ Many residents, especially those living close to the city center and in the remote ger areas, would prefer to live in apartments. However, a significant number of residents, especially in the Midtier ger area, want to keep their existing housing but with improved living conditions and better infrastructure and services.

Ger residents seem to prefer small concentrations of low-rise, multifamily apartment buildings, as opposed to large concentrations of high-rise buildings.

◻ The real estate market is still forming in Mongolia. Housing prices seem to be determined on an ad hoc basis, though there are some consistent correlations between location and housing price, and between dwelling type and housing price.

◻ Housing in the ger areas is financed mostly through private savings. Even for residents who have steady incomes and could afford to purchase apartments, getting loans from commercial banks at an affordable rate would be a key challenge. This difficulty is because bank loans are scarce and because both credit and the mortgage market are still evolving.

◻ A majority of residents in the three ger areas will not be able to afford any of the apartment buildings the government proposes to build. Given the affordability issue, low-cost housing or low-income public rental housing or both should be further examined as alternatives.

Implications for Households in the City Center Ger (Naran): Under the government's plan, some parts of this khoroo will be converted to high-density apartment complexes. An affordability analysis shows that income level, asset holdings, and savings in Naran are not significantly different from those of residents already living in apartments.[5] If the area is converted to apartment complexes targeted for middle-income households, most of the residents in detached houses should be able to afford newly built apartments, if they wish, since they share similar socioeconomic characteristics as residents of the city center (see table 3.13). Even so, these residents would need to finance about 10 to 20 percent of the cost using bank loans. Thus, the lack of a mature credit market could become a key constraint for them.

Residents living in gers, however, face a different story. Their income levels and asset values are only about 70 percent and 40 percent, respectively, of those for residents of detached houses. Ger

TABLE 3.13. Income, Assets, and Housing Prices in City Center Ger

	DWELLING TYPE	AVERAGE MONTHLY INCOME (Tg)	AVERAGE MONTHLY SAVINGS (Tg)	TOTAL ASSETS (MILLION Tg)	CURRENT HOUSING PRICE (MILLION Tg)
City Center ger (Naran)	Ger	257,600	92,400	22.69	1.91
	Detached house	376,600	93,800	53.57	28.97
	Apartment	488,600	204,400	80.62	61.23
Apartment area	Apartment	446,600	29,400	38.93	43.11

Source: World Bank Task Team Survey 2009.
Note: Housing price is benchmarked as average price of apartments in City Center and apartment areas.

residents will be less able to afford apartments. For residents in areas scheduled to be converted, the affordability issue will not be of great importance because developers are likely to compensate them by granting them apartments in exchange for their land.

In newly built apartment areas in Naran, the financial burden of maintenance and operation for housing and other utilities will increase greatly. For detached houses, the annual cost per square meter of maintenance and operation ranges from about Tg 1,400 to Tg 7,000 (US$1 to US$5); maintaining a ger costs practically nothing. When residents move into apartments, their costs would rise to Tg 9,800 to Tg 12,600 (US$7 to US$9) per square meter per year.

Implications for Households in the Midtier and Fringe Gers: Socioeconomic conditions in these two ger areas are much worse than in the City Center ger and apartment areas. The current market price of apartments—ranging from Tg 42 million to Tg 63 million (US$30,000 to US$45,000)—is clearly beyond the affordability range for ger residents whose average monthly income is about Tg 230,000 (US$165) (see table 3.14). These residents will probably have to stay in their existing houses, even if they wish to move to apartments.

TABLE 3.14. Income, Assets, and Housing Prices in Midtier and Fringe Gers

	DWELLING TYPE	AVERAGE MONTHLY INCOME (Tg)	AVERAGE MONTHLY SAVINGS (Tg)	TOTAL ASSETS (MILLION Tg)	CURRENT HOUSING PRICE (MILLION Tg)
Midtier ger	Ger	190,400	4,200	8.74	—
	Detached house	225,400	26,600	24.83	17.59
Fringe ger	Ger	232,400	—	6.96	1.00
	Detached house	225,400	16,800	21.37	18.69

Source: World Bank Task Team Survey 2009.

In the case of the Midtier ger (Bayankhoshuu), a majority of people responded that they are relatively content with their housing conditions and would like to see improvements in the living environment, rather than move to new homes. Hence, maintaining the status quo on housing does not seem much of a concern for them. Residents of the Fringe ger, however, would prefer to move into apartments but, because of their poor economic conditions, will probably have to accept the more realistic alternatives of building or improving their gers and detached houses.

4 Water Supply

STATUS OF CURRENT WATER SUPPLY IN GER AREAS

Water kiosks: The current status of water supply and sewer services is fairly consistent across the three khoroos under review. No house or ger in any ger area of Ulaanbaatar (UB) has a private connection to water distribution networks. Residents instead purchase water at kiosks. More than 550 kiosks have been developed across the ger areas of UB, some 460 of which are managed by Water Supply and Sewage Authority Company of UB City (USUG)—the public water supply and sanitation utility company owned by the municipality of UB (MUB).[1] The rest are contracted out to private operators. About 66 percent of the kiosks depend on tanker trucks operated by USUG for water delivery; most of the rest are connected to water distribution mains, which have been developed under the two World Bank–financed UB Services Improvement Projects. A small number of kiosks in remote areas depend on local water wells. (See appendix D for the distribution of kiosks.[2])

Access to kiosks: Kiosks have been located so that each serves about 900–1,200 people, in line with the city's benchmark of 1,000 people per kiosk. For most residents, kiosks are located within 100–500 meters. Table 4.1 summarizes the distributions of kiosks in the three khoroos under review, and appendix D provides information on broader ger areas.

Services: The selling schedule is generally 10 a.m.–8 p.m., with a midday lunch break. Residents report that 83 percent of kiosks provide water according to this schedule, with exceptions usu-

PHOTO 4.1. Residents fill water containers at a water kiosk.

(Photo by Brett Sedgewick, World Bank)

TABLE 4.1. Distribution of Kiosks in Three Ger Areas

GERS/KHOROOS	PIPE-FED KIOSKS	TRUCK-FED KIOSKS	NUMBER OF RESIDENTS PER KIOSK	DISTANCE FROM KIOSK (M) FOR MOST RESIDENTS
City Center ger (Naran)	9	1	1,225	500 m
Midtier ger (Bayankhoshuu)	9	0	887	100 m
Fringe ger (Sharhad)	5	5	1,113	500 m

Source: USUG (Water Supply and Sewage Authority Company of Ulaanbaatar City) 2009.

ally caused by supply breakdowns or by kiosk employees not following the schedules; 88 percent indicated that this schedule was suitable.[3] Kiosks fed by tanker trucks are less reliable because of limited capacity, breakdowns, and traffic. While it is cumbersome for residents to transport 10–30 liters of water from kiosks to their houses a couple times a week, most of them accept the current practice. Approximately three-quarters use carts for transport, while 2 percent (mostly those living more than 600m from a kiosk) use vehicles.[4] Water transport is made difficult by the weather and the lack of infrastructure: rocky or icy surfaces, speeding traffic, trash-strewn roads, and steep inclines are the most frequently described obstacles.[5] Even so, residents are relatively content with the water supply situation, as compared to other more pressing problems such as the lack of solid waste collection, drainage, and proper sanitation facilities.

PHOTO 4.2. Young children load water for transport.

(Photo by Tomoko Hirai, World Bank/Tokyo)

Affordability: Affordability of water purchased at kiosks is not a significant issue for residents. Household expenditures for water represent less than 3 percent of ger residents' average income, even though that income is quite meager: around Tg 657,000 (US$469) per year for the lowest quintile. Residents can afford water because their consumption is extremely limited: around 5–10 liters per person per day as a result of inconvenient transportation. The water tariff at kiosks is Tg 1,000 (US$0.71) per cubic meter, or Tg 1 (less than US$0.01) per liter. The cost of water, type of dwelling, or household income levels do not seem to affect per capita consumption.[6] Table 4.2 presents detailed data on water expenditures compared to income.

Utility company: USUG is the water supply and sewerage company in charge of developing, maintaining, and operating kiosks, except for about 90 kiosks that have been contracted out to private operators. For USUG, kiosks lose money because the existing tariff of Tg 1,000 (US$0.71) per cubic meter is well under the full unit cost of kiosk water supply operations, which is estimated at somewhere between Tg 3,200 to Tg 4,300 (US$2.29 to US$3.07) per cubic meter, depending on the types of water delivery (truck-fed or piped) and the complexity of construction. Providing water at kiosks is estimated to be more than 10 times more expensive than the cost of central water supply to apartments (Tg 280, or US$0.20, per cubic meter[7]). Each kiosk incurs annual losses in the range of Tg 10 million to Tg 26 million (about US$7,100 to US$18,600), depending on sales volume, which resulted in USUG annual operating losses of Tg 4.1 billion (US$2.9 million) in 2008.[8] The biggest portion of kiosk operating costs is for the salaries of kiosk operating personnel: estimated at 51 percent of the total unit cost of piped kiosks and 44 percent of truck-fed kiosks.[9] For truck-fed kiosks, fuel and operating costs of tanker trucks represent more

TABLE 4.2. Household Water Expenditure and Income

INCOME QUINTILE	HH INCOME (Tg/YEAR)	HH EXPENDITURE ON KIOSK WATER (Tg/YEAR)	PERCENT OF INCOME (HH SURVEY RESPONDENTS)
5th	5,389,809	16,897	0.3%
4th	2,963,326	16,466	0.6%
3rd	2,075,552	14,706	0.7%
2nd	1,412,200	16,764	1.2%
1st	657,144	18,582	2.8%
Total	2,496,897	16,701	0.7%

Source: NSO 2008.

than 30 percent of the unit cost. For pipe-fed kiosks, depreciation charges (or debt service) of the distribution pipe network are 25 percent of total unit costs. More details are reviewed by specific ger areas below.

Wastewater: There is no sewerage service in ger areas since the sewer network has not reached beyond the central apartment areas. Disposal of wastewater in ger areas is not a major issue for now, but it will have to be resolved in the long run. Because of the minimal amount of water consumption in the ger areas and the extreme climate of the country, sewer collection would face almost unsolvable technical challenges unless the ger residential areas are converted to fully served apartment dwellings. Therefore, wastewater issues are only lightly discussed in this report.

Sanitation: Most households have pit latrines, the majority of which are not ventilated. Lined latrines are used to a varying degree from khoroo to khoroo. (See table 4.3 for a breakdown of latrine types.[10]) Although various donors offer programs to improve latrines, none of those programs seem to have made any large-scale impact in ger areas, and some donors have withdrawn support for improved latrines. It does not appear that there is much incentive for ger area residents to invest in improving latrines either. Because of the extremely cold climate of the country, existing programs have proven difficult to adopt in UB or have been very costly. However, the negative environmental impact—pollution of soils and groundwater and the poor health conditions of ger residents—is obvious and will require more focused attention. Because of the current lack of a clear solution, the household sanitation issue is not addressed in this report.

CITY CENTER GER (NARAN), 11TH KHOROO, BAYANGOL DISTRICT

Options of service improvement

A large-scale development of apartment buildings is expected given the proximity of the khoroo to the city center. If apartment buildings are built, they will be connected to the water supply mains. All the apartments will have tap water, as well as hot water, supply.

Costs of water supply and wastewater service to apartment buildings

Water supply mains and sewer collectors already exist near this area, therefore the capital costs of connecting new apartment complexes to the existing service will be minimal. A preliminary development plan prepared by the MUB envisages development of apartment complexes for some 2,450 households, as well as commercial and community infrastructure near this area. It would cost only an estimated Tg 1,855 billion (US$1,325 million) to connect those apartment complexes to the existing water supply mains and wastewater collectors; installing booster pumps would cost around Tg 770,000 (US$550) per household.

TABLE 4.3. Types of Sanitation Facilities

GER TYPE	VENTILATED		LINED	
	YES	NO	YES	NO
City Center (Naran) *Ger*	29.2%	70.8%	64.6%	35.4%
Mid-tier (Bayankhoshuu) *Ger*	42.1%	57.9%	31.6%	68.4%
Fringe*	46.8%	53.2%	58.4%	41.6%

* Data for Bayanzurkh District, 9th Khoroo not available; neighboring 10th Khoroo used.

PHOTO 4.3. Resident uses a water kiosk in the ger areas.

(Photo by Takuya Kamata, World Bank)

Key assumptions are as follows: The total water consumption in these complexes would be 3,350 m³ per day (270 liters per day per capita, which is in line with the current average consumption of apartment residents). Pipeline length is 3.1 km for water supply and 3.4 km for sewer collectors, and pipe diameters are DN100 to DN500 for water supply and DN250 to DN400 for wastewater. The costs of pipes, fittings, and water meters within the apartment buildings are not included in this estimate and will be included in the selling prices of the apartments.

The estimated unit operating cost of the water supply, including maintenance, is the same as the on-going costs of the water supply for existing apartment buildings in the city, estimated at Tg 280 (US$0.20) per cubic meter. The water supply tariff for apartment residents is currently Tg 167 (US$0.12) per cubic meter, which is well below the unit cost of supply. This subsidy causes enormous financial deficits for the water utility company, USUG.

Financial and economic implications of service improvement

Consumer economic benefits: Apartment residents are known to consume large quantities of water because it is heavily subsidized and usage is not metered. The consumption at the new apartment complexes is expected to remain at around 270 liters per person per day, as currently observed in many apartments. This amount would represent a drastic increase over the current water consumption of current ger area residents, who use only about 5 to 10 liters per person per day. Therefore, while the residents of the new apartment complexes are unlikely to be the same current residents of this khoroo, there will be a significant increase in consumer benefits.

Financial implications: The pricing of the water supply for apartments will remain the most critical policy issue. If the current level of heavily subsidized tariffs continues and water consumption increases drastically, the financial performance of the already money-losing water supply operations in UB will be worsened to a calamitous level. Current financial losses of USUG from apartment residential operations are estimated at Tg 41 billion (US$29.3 million) for 2008.

Fiscal implications: Mainly because of significant delays in tariff adjustments for apartments, the USUG is not in a position to service debt obligations on various foreign loans, including subsidiary loans and loans from World Bank USIP1 and USIP2 and from the Spanish government. The outstanding debt obligations amount to some Tg 42 billion (US$30 million). Currently, the MUB is making debt repayments and interest payments on behalf of USUG, thus subsidizing the company's financial losses. If tariff increases are not enacted and water consumption increases in new apartment development, the implicit subsidies also will increase, thus having a significant negative effect on the fiscal performance of the MUB.

Other implications

If additional water sources need to be developed (along with the necessary infrastructure), additional costs will be incurred, though not attributable only to the conversion of houses to apartment buildings. Also, while it is difficult to quantify at this stage, the opportunity costs to the environment of tapping into precious water resources will have to be considered.

There also may be implications for the capacity of the wastewater treatment plant (WWTP) of USUG, because the water consumption volume in this area will significantly increase at the new apartment complexes. There is only one large-scale WWTP in UB with a peak flow of 180,000 m^3 per day, as well as a couple of small independent treatment facilities, including one near the UB international airport.

MIDTIER GER (BAYANKHOSHUU), 8TH KHOROO, SONGINO KHAIRKHAN DISTRICT

Options for service improvement

Some higher-income residents may wish to obtain private water supply connections for their houses. Other affluent residents might wish to consolidate their land plots and to build small-scale residential structures for multiple family dwellings. However, insulating water pipes to protect them from freezing temperatures will be a daunting engineering challenge, and the engineering viability of private connection needs further review. So far, there have been no private water connections to any houses in UB. In addition, wastewater branches will have to be connected to the nearest sewer network. If no sewer network serves the area, other methodologies such as minitreatment plants will have to be pursued.

Cost of service improvement

Several engineering estimates indicate that private connection costs for houses in ger areas would be in the range of Tg 5.6 million to Tg 16.1 million (US$4,000 to US$11,500) per household, excluding in-house materials such as sinks and faucets. The cost depends on many factors in each area, including proximity to the existing water supply networks, connectivity to sewer treatment systems, and topography.

The breakdown of costs is as follows: Construction cost of branches for water distribution and sewer collection and main networks for water and sewer per household amounts to about Tg 5.6

FIGURE 4.1. Examples of House Connection Costs

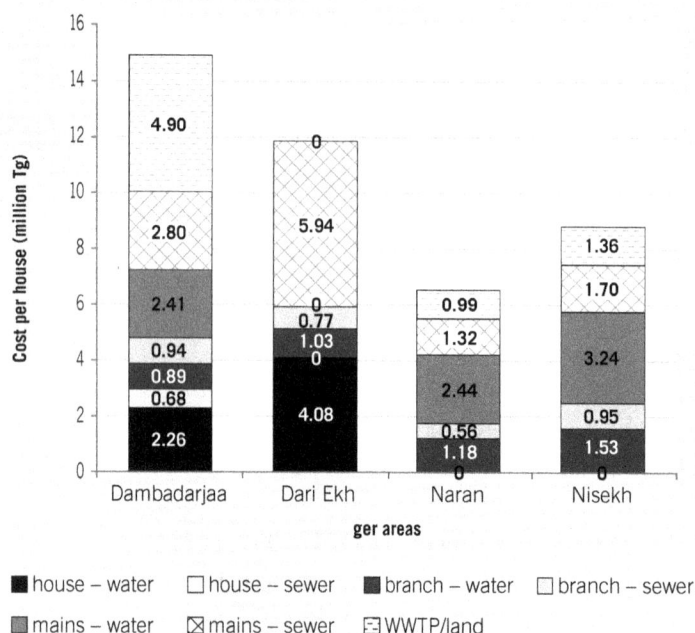

Source: USUG 2009, Second Ulaanbaatar Service Improvement Project, Project Management Unit of Ulaanbaatar City (USIP2 PMU) 2009.

million to Tg 7 million (US$4,000 to US$5,000 per household), excluding construction costs within each private property. The additional cost of connecting to houses within their private property would be around Tg 2.8 million to Tg 4.2 million (US$2,000 to US$3,000) per household. This range means, typically, the total private connection cost will be around Tg 8.4 million to Tg 11.2 million (US$6,000–US$8,000). If a small wastewater facility has to be built because the wastewater main networks have not reached the area, the capital development cost of the independent small wastewater treatment plant will be an additional Tg 4.2 million to Tg 4.9 million (US$3,000–US$3,500) per household. Thus, the total cost in more expensive cases of private connection will be around Tg 12.6 million to Tg 16.1 million (US$9,000 to US$11,500) per household. Details of the breakdown of capital cost for private connection are presented in figure 4.1.

Because there is no existing water supply tariff for individual houses, tariffs for water consumption would be set at somewhere between the current apartment water tariff (currently Tg 167, or US$0.12, per cubic meter) and the ger area kiosk water tariff (currently Tg 1,000, or US$0.71, per cubic meter). Assuming that consumption would increase to 70–80 liters per capita per day, monthly water bills are estimated to be around Tg 19,000 to Tg 115,000 (US$13 to US$82) per four-person household per year.

Affordability and willingness-to-pay for house connections would be major issues, as the average annual income of even the wealthiest quintile of ger residents is Tg 5.4 million, or US$3,600. Options for consideration might include cost-sharing and public contributions to the cost of connecting each private service to the distribution and collection networks. Even if the costs are shared or subsidized at the beginning, consumers might eventually be required pay all the costs through their tariffs.

Benefits of service improvement

Consumer economic benefits: The direct benefit to consumers will be quite significant because the household consumption will definitely increase from the current level of 5–10 liters per person per day to as much as 60–70 liters per person per day—more than a 10-fold increase in some cases.

Utility company: The city-owned utility company (USUG) could recover its costs if private houses are required to pay the actual cost of water delivery and ongoing operations. But if the current, heavily subsidized apartment residential tariff is applied to private houses, USUG will incur substantial losses.

Fiscal implication: Also, depending on who bears the cost of connecting private plots to the water distribution mains (either in the form of direct counterpart contribution at the time of construction, or through tariff collection later on), this expansion of service could put a fiscal burden on the municipality.

Other implications

In the long run, providing piped-in water service to many more homes will require expansion of the city's sewer network and wastewater treatment capacity.

FRINGE GER (SHARHAD), 9TH KHOROO, BAYANZÜRKH DISTRICT

Options for service improvement

Construction of more tanker-fed kiosks with more reliable water delivery is desired for the short term. In the long run, construction of a water main might be considered for connecting the kiosks to water supply mains, depending on the relative costs and benefits of the two options (tanker-fed kiosks or network-connected kiosks).

Cost of service improvement

The cost of building kiosks is relatively small: Tg 12.6 million (US$9,000) per kiosk. However, both pipe-fed kiosks and truck-served kiosks are relatively expensive to operate. This is because of the high cost of personnel required to operate both types of kiosks, the high fuel and operating costs for water tanker trucks for the truck-fed kiosks, and the capital construction cost of the water distribution network for the pipe-fed kiosks. The capital costs of network construction and of rehabilitation or construction of kiosks are presented in table 4.4.

Total unit costs for the networked (pipe-fed) kiosk water supply are estimated at around Tg 3,280 to Tg 4,260 per m^3, compared to the unit cost of central apartment water supply operations of (Tg 280 per m^3). Depending on construction methods and cost calculation methods (for example, attribution of associated central network operation costs and allocation of capital investment costs), the unit costs of the piped-kiosk water supply seem to be lower or equal to the unit cost of trucked-kiosk water supply. According to the 2008 performance indicator calculations made by USUG, the unit cost of the piped-kiosk water supply was Tg 3,280 (US$2.34) per cubic meter (excluding USIP2-related capital costs) and the unit cost of trucked-kiosk water supply was Tg 4260 (US$3.04) per cubic meter. A World Bank task team has estimated that the unit cost of piped-kiosk water supply is around Tg 4,250 (US$3.04) per cubic meter (with fully

TABLE 4.4. Capital Costs of Network/Kiosk Construction[a]

GER AREAS	CAPITAL COSTS (MILLION Tg)	# OF KIOSKS
Bayankhoshuu North	Tg 6,638	36
Bayankhoshuu South	Tg 1,954	29
Chingeltei	Tg 1,712	24
Dari-Ekh	Tg 959	16
Dambadarja	Tg 2,259	26
Total	Tg 13,524	131

Sources: USUG 2009; USIP2 PMU 2009.
[a] USUG 2009, World Bank UISP2 Project

TABLE 4.5. Unit Cost Estimates of Kiosk Water Supply (Tg per m³)

	TRUCKED TO KIOSK	NETWORKED TO KIOSK
USUG estimates	4,260	3,280
WB task team estimates	4,250	4,260

Sources: USUG 2009; USIP2 PMU 2009; COWI 2009.

loaded USIP2-related capital costs), and the unit cost of trucked-kiosk water supply is around Tg 4,260 (US$3.04) per cubic meter (table 4.5).

Conversion of truck-supplied kiosks to networked or piped kiosks would make sense only if a drastic increase in consumption is expected, because the cost advantage for networked kiosks is only marginally proven compared with the cost of truck-supplied kiosks. However, it should be noted that either type of kiosk water supply is very costly when compared to piped-in water supply for apartments. Even with the increased tariff of Tg 1,000 (US$0.71) per cubic meter, kiosk water supply is a huge money-losing operation for the utility company.

Benefits of service improvement

Consumer economic benefits: Converting kiosks from service by trucks to service by networked pipes will have little impact on consumption and, therefore, should not be seen as a direct benefit to consumers.

Financial implications: For USUG, kiosks will remain money-losing operations with the current level of tariff at Tg 1,000 (US$0.71) per cubic meter. The more kiosks are built, the bigger the losses will be. The financial loss of one kiosk for a khoroo is estimated at Tg 19million (about US$13,600) per year, and there are more than 550 kiosks in UB.

Fiscal implications: USUG will not be able to meet debt repayment obligations for the construction of water mains and kiosks as long as the current level of tariffs prevails. Therefore, the MUB will have to assume the debt repayment obligations of USUG.

5 Municipal Roads and Public Transportation

CURRENT STATUS OF ROADS IN CITY CENTER, MIDTIER, AND FRINGE GERS

The condition of road networks in the three khoroos reviewed in this study is largely similar. Most of the roads began as informal tracks to hashaas and ger households under development. As subsequent hashaas were plotted out and land taken, tracks were simply extended to reach them. There was no formal planning involved, and with time the tracks evolved in a haphazard manner to become earthen roads. As a result, they have little connectivity or integration with the formal municipal road network.

The earthen roads in each of the khoroos have no predetermined alignments, are not built to any standards, lack consistent dimensions, and are completely devoid of supporting facilities, including drainage systems, sidewalks, and space for parking. Street lights are evident along some of the roads, but many do not work and others are unreliable. Along any given corridor, the width of available rights-of-way ranges from about 2.5 meters to 16 meters, and the roads often have sudden and unexpected sharp turns. The roads are suitable only for smaller vehicles because larger ones are unable to negotiate the unforeseen narrow passages and tight turns. In some instances, the earthen roads end abruptly at certain geographic features, such as deep ravines, gullies, or steep hillsides.

Except during the rainy season, vehicles driving along the earthen roads create dust. When it does rain, the roads turn to mud. Because there is no proper drainage, water flows from the surrounding slopes onto the roadway. This runoff accelerates deterioration and creates a nuisance for people living in the area. During winter months, the snow and ice on steeper slopes can create treacherous driving conditions. Residents complained of having to wash clothes and shoes more than normal because of the earthen roads.

PHOTO 5.1. Truck approaches on an earthen road in the Midtier ger (Bayankhoshuu)

(Photo by Takuya Kamata, World Bank)

Shallow ravines are common in ger areas, and it is not unusual for those ravines to be used as roads during dry periods. Typically, hashaas are situated along both sides of a ravine with fences built to the edge. During heavy rains or prolonged wet periods, the ravines flood, thereby cutting off a route for vehicles. The rains also bring trash and garbage onto roadways, creating health hazards.

Approximately 10 percent of the road network in the three gers is paved. However, most of the paved networks tend to be large arterial roads that border the gers. The short segments of secondary paved road that penetrate the gers tend to be in very poor condition and have deteriorated so much that they need to be reconstructed. Most roads have a Present Serviceability Rating (PSR) roughness[1] of between 1 and 2, which means they are passable but not in good condition. The exceptions to this condition are located in the City Center ger (Naran), in which there is a 1.5 km stretch of paved road that bisects the ger area, and a short segment of Khasbaatariin Street, both of which are in good condition. Although the districts are responsible for maintaining khoroo roads, preventive maintenance is almost never undertaken. Table 5.1 provides a snapshot of road type by length in each of the gers included in this study.

If one excludes the City Center ger, the percentage of paved roads drops significantly to just over 3 percent.

CURRENT STATUS OF PUBLIC TRANSPORTATION

Greater Ulaanbaatar Area: The public transportation system in Ulaanbaatar (UB) consists of large buses, trolley buses, minibuses, and taxis. According to estimates,[2] there are more than 155 million passenger trips per year, which equates to an average of around 435,000 passenger trips daily.

Public transportation services are essential for enhancing people's mobility and access to work, school, and other activities. In the greater UB area, passenger transportation demand consists of buses (34 percent), walking (30 percent), cars (25 percent), taxis (9 percent), and other (2 percent). The most popular mode of travel to work is by bus (39 percent), while 85 percent of students walk or use the bus to get to school. The average time it takes to get to work is 32 minutes, and the average distance traveled is 4.5 km.

Large buses typically seat between 40 and 50 passengers, while minibuses have seating for 12 to 15 passengers. Bus fares, which are set by the municipality, are Tg 300 (US$0.21) for large buses, between Tg 200 ($0.14) and Tg 400 (US$0.29) for minibuses (depending on distance traveled), and Tg 400 (US$0.29) per km for taxis. However, with only around 25 percent of passengers paying

TABLE 5.1. Road Type by Ger

TYPE OF ROAD	CITY CENTER GER	MIDTIER GER	FRINGE GER	TOTAL
Earthen	18,461	23,241	30,611	72,313
Paved	6,805	1,004	807	8,616
Totals	25,266	24,245	31,418	80,929
% Paved roads	26.9	4.1	2.6	10.6

Source: JICA 2009.
Note: The figures above are in meters unless otherwise specified.

the full price on large buses, the government is obliged to heavily subsidize fares. Nearly 100 percent of passengers using minibuses pay full fare.

City Center, Midtier and Fringe Khoroos: With the exception of the Sharhad bus station,[3] which is on the edge of the khoroo boundary in the Fringe ger, only minibuses and taxis provide service to the three gers. However, services are limited by the poor road quality, an inability to access all areas during inclement weather, and the drivers' unfamiliarity with the destinations within the gers. In each of the three khoroos under study, approximately 20 percent or fewer households own vehicles.[4] As a result, the share of walking is high among families that do not own a vehicle, and the use of public transportation is high among all households. The use of bicycles and motorbikes is not common.

Rough estimates indicate that inhabitants of the three gers get to work using public transportation services (buses) 58 percent of the time, followed by walking (29 percent) and family vehicles (13 percent). Those figures would indicate that residents rely almost twice as much on public transportation (buses) to travel to work as do citizens of other districts (34 percent), and that they use private vehicles half as much (13 percent vs. 25 percent). The average travel time to work (25 minutes) is roughly the same as for residents of other districts, but the average distance traveled (8 km) is almost twice as far. Because residents rely heavily on public transportation to get to work, initiatives to improve bus services to the khoroos should be considered.

In terms of traveling to school, 90 percent of students in the three gers walk the entire way or walk to catch a bus; this number is in line with findings for students in other districts. However, it takes twice as long to get to school (16 minutes more) in these gers than in other districts, even though the distance is nearly 1 km less on average. Because so many students walk to school, construction of sidewalks and adequate street lighting are important priorities.

During informal interviews with 21 minibus driver or owners who currently provide services to the peripheries of the khoroos, all indicated that they would expand services *within* the khoroos if roads were widened and improved (that is, paved).

Tables 5.2 and 5.3 provide snapshots of transportation modes and travel times and distances for all districts in UB and for the three khoroos in this study.

A casual observation of traffic counts[5] at select key intersections in each of the targeted ger areas reveals that in the City Center (Naran) and Midtier (Bayankhoshuu) gers, the overwhelming percentage of vehicles observed were passenger cars (table 5.4). In the Fringe ger (Naran), more than half of the vehicles were buses, presumably because the Sharhad bus station is located in the south-central edge of the ger.

TABLE 5.2. Transportation Modes in UB

TRANSPORTATION DEMAND BY MODE	ULAANBAATAR	TARGETED GER AREAS
Bus	34%	58%
Walk	30%	29%
Family vehicle	25%	13%

Source: World Bank Task Team Survey 2009.

TABLE 5.3. Travel Times and Distances in UB and Ger Areas

TRAVEL TIMES AND DISTANCES	ULAANBAATAR	TARGETED GER AREAS
To work (averages)	32 mins./ 4.5 km	25 mins./ 8.0 km
To school (averages)	27 mins./ 3.3 km	43 mins./ 2.5 km

Source: World Bank Task Team Survey 2009.

TABLE 5.4. Observed Vehicles in Targeted Ger Areas

DISTRICT	CARS	%	BUSES	%	TRUCKS	%
City Center ger	48,391	93	933	2	2,523	5
Midtier ger	7,335	87	130	2	976	11
Fringe ger	407	26	828	52	351	22
Totals	56,133		1,891		3,850	

Source: World Bank Task Team Survey 2009.

OPTIONS AND CHALLENGES FOR SERVICE IMPROVEMENTS

Options: Road quality and safe access for pedestrians seem to be the biggest concerns for residents of the three khoroos. When asked what measures were most needed to improve transportation in their khoroo, 95 percent of respondents supported the improvement of district roads and of conditions for pedestrians.[6] Because the roads are too rough for most public transportation operators to provide comprehensive service, many residents must walk long distances—up to 30 minutes in some cases—to reach their homes. In doing so, they must compete with vehicles for the limited space available, and they say that after dark, the lack of street lighting contributes to crime.[7] Improving roads would also facilitate access for emergency vehicles, including ambulances and fire trucks, as well as the delivery of goods and other services.

Increasing the coverage and frequency of public bus services is another priority area. When residents were asked what measures would improve the current transportation situation in the three khoroos, more than 95 percent of inhabitants wanted improvements to bus and taxi stops.[8] When asked to assess the quality of minibus services in terms of convenience of transfer to other city buses, 45 percent responded that it was "bad" or "very bad."[9]

Challenges: One of the key reasons operators do not provide service to these areas is the extremely poor condition of roads, which prevents them from entering many areas. Improving road quality would encourage public transportation providers to extend their operations in the three khoroos, and it would appear that demand is high for public transportation services in those areas. While paving roads would increase access, it would also have a dramatic impact on area development, both in terms of land use and socioeconomic activity. As such, any plans to pave or build roads in the khoroos must be considered in light of local land-use plans.

If roads are to be paved, facilities for pedestrians, including sidewalks and street lighting, must be included. It would also make sense to consider preserving the rights-of-way for possible future utility services (power, water, and wastewater), although this provision could involve considerable additional expense. However, because of the significant cost involved, the provision of water supply and sanitation services should be considered only if there are apartment blocks along a paved road's alignment. If public transportation services were to be extended into the khoroos, space would also be needed to construct lay-bys for public transportation stops.

Another difficulty to paving roads in the khoroos is the likelihood that land will need to be acquired from property owners. Because there was no formal planning in the location of hashaas, plots are of various sizes. As a result, most of the earthen roads do not have straight alignments. Instead, they meander past and around hashaas and natural geographic features. Complicating matters are the fences that most owners have built to enclose their hashaas, many of which extend into the path of the earthen roads. Depending on the alignment of the road to be paved, some inhabitants or economic activities might need to be relocated.

Maintaining the improved roads would present another challenge. The value of maintaining roads has long been recognized. For example, roads in good condition reduce vehicle operating costs, decrease travel times, and contribute to safe driving conditions. International good practice calls for countries to spend about 1 percent of their GDP to maintain existing roads. For Mongolia, which had an estimated GDP of around US$3 billion in 2008, this practice would imply expenditures in the range of US$30 million per year. However, only Tg 4.2 billion (US$3 million), or about 0.1 percent of GDP, was spent to maintain the country's network of roads in 2008. Any plan for road improvements will require a review of options for financing the cost of maintenance.

All road projects would need to be carefully reviewed and subjected to a variety of technical assessments. Those evaluations would include geotechnical studies and hydrological reviews, as well as economic, financial, environmental, and social analyses to ensure their viability and value for money.

Construction and Maintenance Costs

Typical Construction Costs:[10] Low traffic-volume roads and parking areas are often sealed using double bituminous surface treatment (rather than hot mix paving) because of the cost savings that are possible.[11] In Ulaanbaatar, the cost to build roads using this method is about Tg 28 million (US$20,000) per km, and the municipality has issued a set of guidelines for using double surface treatment for ger area roads.[12] To drain storm water from the road surface and the base course, U-shaped roadside ditches, lined with stones in concrete, are proposed at a cost of approximately Tg 70 million (US$50,000) per km.[13]

The cost to build concrete sidewalks (1 meter wide) is about Tg 21,000 (US$15) per square meter, and the cost to erect street lighting is around Tg 420,000 (US$300) per streetlight.[14] There would be an additional cost of some Tg 14 million (US$10,000) per km for cabling and control boxes.[15]

Typical Maintenance Costs: As a general guideline, countries should devote about 1 percent of GDP annually to maintain road assets. In Mongolia, this amount would equate to about Tg 840,000 (US$600) per km per year[16]. The average estimated amount spent to maintain and power street lighting in each of Ulaanbaatar's khoroos is Tg 2.1 million (US$1,500) per month.

City Center Ger (Naran): 11th Khoroo, Bayangol District

Roads: The khoroo covers some 162 hectares, has 12,245 inhabitants, and is characterized by hilly terrain. The khoroo has about 25.3 km of roads, 6.8 km of which are paved. The percentage of paved roads is higher in this ger than the other two locations under study (27 percent compared to 4 percent and 2 percent), and the roads tend to be in better condition. However, most of the paved network runs along the eastern and southern periphery. There are also three vehicular bridges and

PHOTO 5.2. A paved road in the City Center Ger

(Photo by Takuya Kamata, World Bank)

eight foot-bridges. In addition, residents have better access to public transportation, because of its central location and dense concentration of inhabitants, than do those in the other areas. It is, however, one of the older ger areas, with even less order in the placement of hashaas and gers. As such, when one leaves the paved network, the streets tend to meander more and are narrower, which creates a challenging environment for vehicular movement.

Because of the hilly nature of this khoroo, and because of the lack of protective measures on the steep slopes, large stones and boulders have been known to roll down the hillsides after heavy rains, thus diminishing road width. During winter months, it is often not possible for vehicles to use the undulating narrow roads that are covered with snow and ice.

An existing 1,200-meter-long floodwater dam was constructed between 1982 and 1985. It is in poor condition, and garbage has accumulated at the dam wall. Illegal ger dwellers occupy the upper end of the floodway.

The city plans to build a series of apartment complexes in the southern half of the khoroo. The plans should provide for sufficient parking for the residents of those apartments.

It is estimated that 5–10 percent of khoroo residents own private vehicles. A quick observation of traffic indicates that this khoroo has the most daily traffic of the three under study. At the ger's busiest intersection, Tasganii Ovoo, the average daily traffic is around 52,000 vehicles per day. The vast majority of vehicles, 93 percent, are passenger cars; buses and microbuses account for less than 2 percent of traffic. This finding indicates that at Tasganii Ovoo intersection, a lot of vehicular traffic originates outside, or passes through, the area.

Public Transportation: Although numerous public transportation options serve the eastern and southern peripheries along main transport corridors, no regular microbus service is offered inside the ger. Taxis provide only limited access, primarily along the east-west road that bisects the khoroo. As a result, residents must typically walk from 100 meters to 500 meters to access public transportation services. Because of the hilly terrain, walking can be particularly challenging during winter, when temperatures regularly drop to −30 degrees Celsius, and during spring, when the rains turn the earthen roads to mud.

Options for Service Improvements: Because of its location in central Ulaanbaatar, the City Center ger has more paved roads and better access to public transportation services than do the other two gers in the study. Nonetheless, improving roads and encouraging better public transportation services remain important considerations. Residents indicated that their priorities would include the following investments:

Option 1: Upgrade and pave (including drainage, sidewalks, and street lighting) the 1.2 km road that runs from the "Micro Road" on the southern periphery and in a northerly direction past the District Center to the "TV bus terminal intersection." This road used to be well maintained and is paved for the first 200 meters off Micro Road. When traffic builds on the main road, drivers use this road as a bypass.

Option 2: Remove the current restrictions that prohibit microbus operators from providing scheduled services along the main paved road that bisects the khoroo from east ("TV bus terminal") to west ("microbus #7 terminal"). Designated areas beside a road where microbuses can pull over and not impede traffic, or bus lay-bys, should be constructed, and sidewalks should be built along the length of the road. Street lighting is already in place.

Option 3: Provide paved sidewalks from the microbus terminal on the southwestern periphery north about 2 km to the kindergarten. This alignment is steep and passes through a high-density area. It was reported that a number of citizens walk along this route because it is too difficult for most vehicles to access.

PHOTO 5.3. Bus service on a main corridor

(Photo by Takuya Kamata, World Bank)

Although parking is not currently planned as an option, it is highly recommended that adequate parking be provided for the residents of the planned apartment complexes. Parking is necessary because of the already high percentage of passenger cars operating in and around the khoroo.

Cost of Service Improvements

The estimated cost of proposed service improvements 1, 2, and 3 are outlined in table 5.5.

TABLE 5.5. Estimated Costs of Proposed Service Improvements in City Center Ger

CITY CENTER GER (NARAN) PROPOSED SERVICE IMPROVEMENT	LENGTH OR QUANTITY	COST/UNIT (MILLION Tg)	COMPONENT COST (MILLION Tg)	PER CAPITA COST (THOUSAND Tg)
1. Upgrade and pave 1.2 km from Micro Rd. to TV bus terminal				
1.1 Road construction (double surface treatment per km)	1.0	28	28	2.3
1.2 Road drainage system (per km)	1.2	70	84	6.9
1.3 Sidewalks (per km)	1.2	21	25.2	2.1
1.4 Street lighting (1 every 50 meters)	20	0.42	22.4	1.8
1.5 Cabling for street lights (per km)	1.2	14	30.8	2.5
Estimated capital cost:			*190.4*	*15.5*
2. Remove restrictions on microbus operators (East-West Rd.)				0.0
2.1 Construct bus lay-bys (per km, 2 each direction)	4	28	112	9.1
2.2 Sidewalks (per km)	1.0	21	21	1.7
Estimated capital cost:			*133*	*10.9*
3. Provide sidewalk from microbus terminal to kindergarten				0.0
3.1 Sidewalks (per km)	2.0	21	42	3.4
Estimated capital cost:			*42*	*3.4*
Overall estimated cost of improvements:			**365.4**	**29.8**

Source: World Bank Task Team estimates 2009.

Financial and Economic Implications of Service Improvements

Economic Benefits to Residents: Benefits for residents would come mainly from improved road conditions (which would make a minor contribution to lowering vehicle operating costs) and from more reliable and higher frequency of bus services (which would decrease travel times for some users by reducing the walking distance to catch a microbus). The sidewalk to the kindergarten would create safer walking conditions. Those improvements would result in increased access to markets, schools, health clinics, other public services, and employment—as well as improved air quality because of a reduction of dust.

Fiscal Implications: Implementing the improvements proposed in this section would have fiscal implications, primarily in the form of funding required to maintain the new assets. The improved road would require routine, periodic maintenance, which is collectively estimated to cost Tg 840,000 (US$600) per km per year (or Tg 1 million/US$720 per year for the proposed road improvement project). If street lighting systems are provided at 50-meter intervals along the improved road, the cost to maintain and power them is expected to be less than Tg 1.1 million (about US$800) per year, Tg 90 (US$0.06) per resident.[17]

Midtier ger (Bayankhoshuu): 8th khoroo, Songino Khairkhan District

Roads: The Midtier khoroo covers an area of nearly 99 hectares of land, is home to 7,979 inhabitants, and has predominately flat terrain. Among the 24.2 km of roads, only 4 percent, or 1 km, are paved. All of the paved roads run along the northern, western, and eastern boundaries of the khoroo. There are no paved roads *within* the khoroo. The most striking feature about the road network in this khoroo is the fact that there is just one north-south road (the "Gully Road") on the western side. However, this road does not provide access to the northern side of the khoroo because it stops some 750 meters short of the main road to the north. All other roads have east-to-west alignments, which severely limit access and vehicular movement. Fences enclosing hashaas abut one another, preventing north-south access, but small footpaths every 1 km or so do permit pedestrians to walk between some hashaas.

Approximately 7 percent of residents own private vehicles. Traffic counts were taken at the intersection between Zuunsalaa and Bayankhoshuu Streets (along the main road bordering the khoroo to the north). A rough estimate of average daily traffic along this stretch is 8,500 vehicles per day. The majority of vehicles, 86 percent, are passenger cars, with buses and microbuses accounting for about 1 percent.

Residents complain of heavy trucks transporting bricks between hashaas where no formal roads exist. The bricks come from factories that operate in the southern side of the khoroo. Trucks operate throughout the day, produce inordinate amounts of dust, plus create hazardous conditions for pedestrians.

Public Transportation: No regular microbus services are provided within the khoroo. To travel within the khoroo, most residents walk or rely on taxis, when available.

Options for Service Improvements: Providing better north-south access is a priority for most residents. Improving the Gully Road would be helpful, but because it's on the western side of the khoroo, another north-south alignment farther to the east should be identified. There are no sidewalks or street lighting on the Gully Road; during the rainy season, low elevations along the alignment tend to have standing water.

Option 1: Upgrade and pave, including drainage, sidewalks, and street lighting, the existing Gully Road from Bayankhoshuu #25 to Nuur Street (about 1.4 km). Some minor changes in the alignment may be required, and, if possible, the road should be extended to the northern side of the khoroo. It is important to note that extending the road might require the acquisition of property, which would add to the cost of the project. It is also worth noting that the overall length of the Gully Road is around 3.7 km and that around 2.3 km of the road passes through two other khoroos (to the northeast and southwest). Any planned improvements to the road should be coordinated with those khoroos.

The estimated cost to improve the Gully Road is summarized in table 5.6.

Financial and Economic Implications of Service Improvements

Economic Benefits to Residents: Although limited to one side of the khoroo, an improved Gully Road would provide a reliable north-south corridor with year-round access. This improve-

TABLE 5.6. Estimated Costs of Proposed Service Improvements in Midtier Ger

MIDTIER GER (BAYANKHOSHUU) PROPOSED SERVICE IMPROVEMENT	LENGTH OR QUANTITY	COST/UNIT (MILLION Tg)	COMPONENT COST (MILLION Tg)	PER CAPITA COST (THOUSAND Tg)
1. Upgrade and extend Gully Road				
1.1 Road construction (double surface treatment per km)	2.1	28	58.8	7.4
1.2 Road drainage system (per km)	2.1	70	147	18.4
1.3 Sidewalks (per km)	2.1	21	44.1	5.5
1.4 Street lighting (1 every 50 meters)	42	0.42	31.64	4.0
1.5 Cabling for street lights (per km)	2.1	14	43.4	5.4
Estimated capital cost:			*324.94*	*40.7*
Overall estimated cost of improvements:			**324.94**	**40.7**

Source: World Bank Task Team estimates 2009.
Note: If the road is not extended 750 meters to the north, the cost would be about Tg 226 million, or US$161,400.

ment would be the biggest benefit to residents. It would speed travel times and might open the way for microbus services. Sidewalks and street lighting would create safer and cleaner walking conditions for pedestrians. Those improvements would also result in increased access to markets, schools, health clinics, other public services, and employment, as well improved air quality because of the reduction of dust.

Fiscal Implications: Financing the costs for routine and periodic maintenance of an improved Gully Road would require about Tg 1.75 million (US$1,250) per year with the extension, and Tg 1.2 million (US$840) per year if the extension is excluded. Maintaining and powering the street lighting system can be expected to cost less than Tg 1.96 million, or US$1,400 annually (Tg 1.26 million, or US$925 without the extension). Per capita, the costs would be about Tg 300 to Tg 465 (US$0.22 to US$0.33) per year.

Fringe Ger (Sharhad): 9th khoroo, Bayanzürkh District

Roads: The Fringe ger is the largest outlying khoroo both in terms of size (48 hectares) and number of inhabitants (11,130). It has the same hilly terrain as the City Center ger and is bordered on the west by the Uliastai River and on the north by the Eej Khairkan (mother mountain). Overall, there are about 31.4 km of roads, 30.6 km of which are earthen (97.5 percent). The 807 meters of paved roads that run from the khoroo boundary to the Sharhad bus station are in very poor condition.

Some 20 percent of residents own private vehicles. Traffic counts were taken of vehicles passing through the main intersection where the National Physiology Health Center is located. According to very limited observations, the average daily volumes seem to be around 1,600 vehicles per day. Buses and microbuses made up just over 50 percent of traffic, followed by passenger cars (25 percent) and trucks (25 percent). The composition of traffic at this location is different from the other khoroos included in this study, where well over 90 percent of traffic consisted of passenger cars. The higher percentage of buses is likely the result of the Sharhad bus station.

PHOTO 5.4. An earthen access road in the ger

(Photo by Takuya Kamata, World Bank)

Public Transportation: The Sharhad bus station is situated on the extreme south-central edge of the khoroo, occupying nearly 650 m² of land. It is used by large buses, minibuses, and taxis. The bus station is located on a roundabout, but is not well organized and creates a bottleneck as drivers seek to enter and exit the facility. It is also located next to a school, which creates unsafe conditions for students.

There are no scheduled bus services or bus stops beyond the Sharhad station, but some taxis do offer to take residents to some outlying areas within the khoroo. However, much of the area has very rough road conditions, which limits where most taxis will go. Residents who need to use public transportation must walk from their homes to the Sharhad bus station or must hope to catch a shared taxi that might be passing by.

Because of its distant location, residents must travel twice as far to get to and from the central business district, which results in higher travel costs for inhabitants of this khoroo.

Options for Service Improvements: Although residents of this hilly khoroo would welcome improved public transportation services, they expressed more interest in having better roads. Many residents provided suggestions for improving specific roads, but most of the proposed projects presented problems. In one case, the road to be improved would provide better access for hashaas that had been built in an illegal area. Proposed road improvements in the core of the khoroo were constrained by limited space and by narrow, winding alignments that would severely limit the size of vehicles that could use the road. As such, only one proposed road improvement project was considered.

Option 1: Upgrade and pave, including drainage, sidewalks, and street lighting, the 1.5 km road from the Sharhad bus station to the top of Eej Khairkan Mountain to the north. The proposed route parallels a high-density area to the west and would provide residents better access on the north side of the khoroo. If conditions were improved, microbus operators might offer bus services for residents in the area along the alignment.

A number of residents also asked that the Sharhad bus station be relocated to the top of Eej Khairkan Mountain because of ample open land that's available. However, doing so would require a significant study to determine the benefits, if any, and the potential environmental and social implications. It would also take considerable coordination with municipal agencies.

The estimated cost to improve the 1.5 km road to Eej Khairkan Mountain is outlined in table 5.7.

Economic and Financial Implications of Service Improvements

Consumer Economic Benefits: If public transportation services are provided along the new route, the biggest economic benefit to residents would likely be the amount of time saved by not having to walk to and from the Sharhad bus station. The improvements would result in increased access to markets, schools, health clinics, other public services, and employment, as well as improved air quality because of the reduction of dust.

Fiscal Implications. Funding maintenance activities would be the biggest fiscal impact. Routine and periodic maintenance for the improved road is estimated to cost Tg 1.26 million (US$900) per year, while the cost to maintain and operate the streetlights would be around Tg 1.4 million (US$1,000) per year. Per capita, those costs would be around Tg 239 (US$0.17) annually.

TABLE 5.7. Estimated Costs of Proposed Service Improvements in Fringe Ger

FRINGE GER (SHARHAD) PROPOSED SERVICE IMPROVEMENT	LENGTH OR QUANTITY	COST/UNIT (MILLION Tg)	COMPONENT (MILLION Tg)	PER CAPITA COST (THOUSAND Tg)
1. Upgrade road from Sharhad bus station to Eej Khairkan				
1.1 Road construction (double surface treatment per km)	1.5	28.00	42.00	3.8
1.2 Road drainage system (per km)	1.5	70.00	105.00	9.4
1.3 Sidewalks (per km)	1.5	21.00	31.50	2.8
1.4 Street lighting (1 every 50 meters)	30	0.42	26.60	2.4
1.5 Cabling for streetlights (per km)	1.5	14.00	35.00	3.1
Estimated capital cost:			*240.10*	*21.6*
Overall estimated cost of improvements:			***240.10***	***21.6***

Source: World Bank Task Team estimates 2009.

6 Solid Waste Management

OVERVIEW OF CURRENT SOLID WASTE MANAGEMENT IN GER AREAS

Institutional Arrangement: The bulk of responsibilities for solid waste management are decentralized to the district level, while the city government is responsible for landfill operations. Until 2007, the City Waste Management Department directly managed the collection and disposal of solid waste in Ulaanbaatar (UB). In 2007, a new regulation on waste management was introduced to minimize the city government's involvement, while increasing the efficiency of management. Under the current institutional arrangement, each district government is responsible for collection and transportation of waste from homes, business entities, and all other locations except for public, spaces. The waste management department of each district collects fees (which are often decided by the city council) (figure 6.1), manages contracting services with a privately run waste collection

FIGURE 6.1. Institutional Arrangement and Responsibilities for Solid Waste Management in Ulaanbaatar

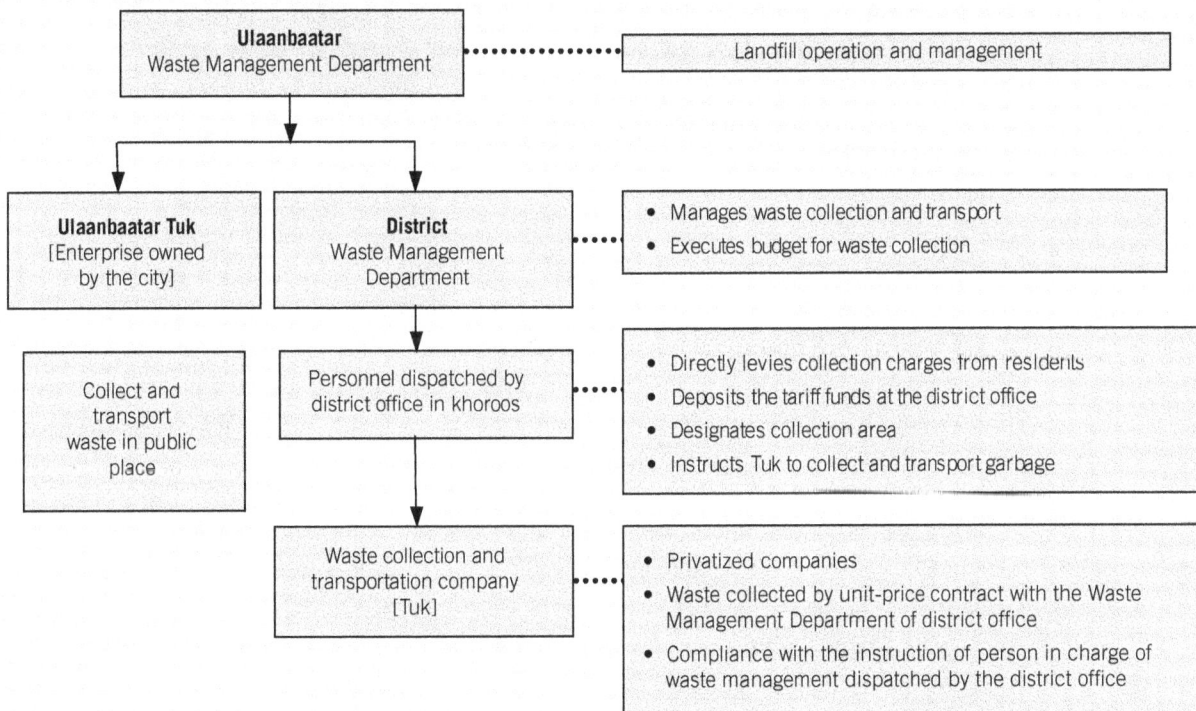

Source: World Bank Task Team 2009.

and transportation company (a *Tuk*), and it provides street cleaning services to citizens. The Waste Management Department of UB operates waste landfills and collects and transports waste in public places by contracting-out to the state-owned enterprise, Ulaanbaatar Tuk.

Current Garbage Collection System: Because formal garbage collection is infrequent and unpredictable, residents dispose of most household waste themselves—usually by dumping it outside their houses, on hills, in yards, and alongside roads and waterways. This ad hoc waste disposal poses a risk to public health and sanitation, including respiratory diseases. Open garbage disposal is also linked to environmental degradation, including the contamination of soil and underground water. In contrast, apartment areas run a relatively efficient and clean system. Separate transfer spaces are installed on the first floor of each building, and waste is discharged into those spaces by trash chutes directly connected to individual apartment units.

Ger area garbage is collected by vehicles that visit each household, door-to-door, and collect fees onsite. In the City Center ger, an autonomous collection system within the khoroo has been put in place. The khoroo owns collection vehicles and operates a few crews of drivers and supporting staff. District staff and vehicles go around to households to collect garbage and to levy the waste collection charge. The district government, in turn, pays a community-owned system for collection and transportation to landfill sites. In the case of the Midtier (Bayankhoshuu) and Fringe (Sharhad), collection is done similarly by collection vehicles visiting each household and transferring the collected garbage to landfill sites (see figure 6.2).

The quantity of waste produced in ger areas varies significantly by season. The waste quantity during winter is three times that of summer: 0.9–1.0 kg per person per day in winter in comparison with 0.2–0.3 kg per person per day in summer. This quantity is because heating fuel (mostly wood and coal) is consumed in large volumes during the cold winters. Ashes are separated from general garbage and usually are discharged into 200-liter iron drums or sacks. During the summer, when fuel is used only for cooking, ash is not separated. Throughout the year, recyclable materials are sorted for sale to the recyclable materials stores.

The frequency of waste collection in the ger areas is very low, from once a month in the case of the Midtier and Fringe gers, to once every three months in the City Center ger (see table 6.1). Low frequency of collection is attributed to a number of factors. First, the current vehicle-based system of collection at each household is not efficient given the low density of ger areas. Collection vehicles can cover only 20–30 households during summer and 15–20 households in winter per two-to-three hour trip. Collection vehicles operate on average nine hours per day; hence, each vehicle can cover fewer than 100 households per day.

A shortage of collection vehicles, equipment, and workers is another problem. District governments have limited resources for equipment and vehicles, because their revenue is solely dependent on a collected tariff. According to the field survey, only one open truck, one driver, and two assistant workers are assigned in each ger area to cover 1,677 to 3,000 households (see Options and Challenges for Service Improvement for detailed investment requirement). Finally, poor road conditions, or in some cases the lack of an access road to ger households, add to the difficulty of collection. Houses located at a distance from the main road, without proper road access or with very narrow roads, often remain unserved.

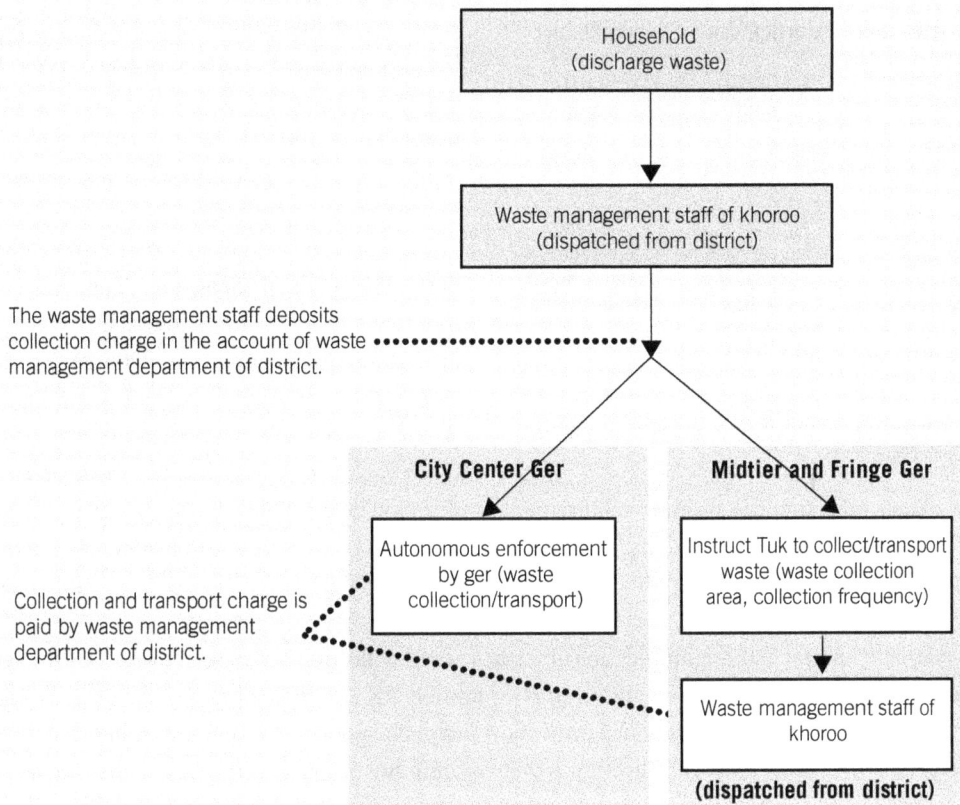

FIGURE 6.2. Solid Waste Collection in Three Ger Areas

```
┌─────────────────────────┐
│      Household          │
│   (discharge waste)     │
└─────────────────────────┘
             │
             ▼
┌─────────────────────────┐
│ Waste management staff  │
│      of khoroo          │
│ (dispatched from        │
│      district)          │
└─────────────────────────┘
```

The waste management staff deposits collection charge in the account of waste ••••••••••••••••• management department of district.

City Center Ger

Autonomous enforcement by ger (waste collection/transport)

Collection and transport charge is paid by waste management department of district.

Midtier and Fringe Ger

Instruct Tuk to collect/transport waste (waste collection area, collection frequency)

Waste management staff of khoroo

(dispatched from district)

Source: World Bank Task Team 2009.

TABLE 6.1. Solid Waste Management in Three Ger Areas

CLASSIFICATION	CITY CENTER GER	MIDTIER GER	FRINGE GER
Households/population	3,000/12,245	1,677/7,979	2,500/11,130
% of HH paying tariff	30%	less than 20%	30%
Frequency of waste collection	2 times/day, 1 time/3 months per household	3 times/day, 1 time/month per household	2 times/day, 1 time/month per household
Form and number of pieces of collection equipment	1 open truck	1 open truck	1 open truck
Number of collectors	1 driver, 2 assistant workers	1 driver, 2 assistant workers	1 driver, 2 assistant workers
Wages of collector (Tg./capita.trip)	driver: 4,500 assistant worker: 4,000	4,000	7,000
Distance to landfill	approx. 15 km	approx. 9 km	approx. 30 km

Sources: Interviews with district officials and khoroo leaders and World Bank Task Team 2009.

TABLE 6.2. Solid Waste Tariff in Three Ger Areas

ITEM	CITY CENTER GER	MIDTIER GER	FRINGE GER
Collection tariff per HH	3,000 Tg/ month	1,500 Tg/ month	2,500 Tg/ month
% of HHs paying tariff	30%	below 20%	30~40%
Willingness of HHs to pay an increased charge for better collection	Additional payment is difficult, because the current waste collection charge is high.	Additional charges could be paid, if collection charges are differentiated for each season.	Current collection charge should be maintained.

Source: World Bank Task Team Interviews 2009.

The collection schedule is random, and there is no designated date and time for collection. Because garbage bins are kept inside household fences, waste cannot be collected if no one is at home. The unpredictability of waste collection reinforces residents' habits of disposing domestic garbage in open dump sites nearby.

Solid Waste Tariff Structure: The waste collection tariff for households in UB was set by the Municipal Council in 2006 at Tg 2,500 (US$1.79) per month for ger areas and Tg 2,000 (US$1.43) per month for apartment residents. However, the district can adjust the tariff level to some extent reflecting the revenue requirements and socioeconomic conditions of ger residents. In the City Center ger (Naran), the monthly tariff is Tg 3,000 (US$2.14); in the Fringe ger (Sharhad), Tg 2,500 (US$1.79); and in the Midtier ger (Bayankhoshuu), Tg 1,500 (US$1.07) (see table 6.2).

Only about 30 percent of households actually pay a waste collection tariff (see table 6.2). One reason obviously is the socioeconomic condition of poor households. Another important factor is the lack of awareness of the need for environmental protection and public goods. The field survey indicates that ger residents generally think garbage collection is the responsibility of city government, so they are not used to the notion of paying for public service. Furthermore, some residents who could afford the collection fee do not want to pay as long as they can dispose of domestic garbage elsewhere outside their houses. Residents also do not seem to have a strong confidence in the government's ability to manage waste. Some long-term residents believe that the garbage problem is created by new migrants and are reluctant to pay the collection fee. When asked about their willingness to pay for improved collection, only the Midtier ger residents showed a willingness to pay additional collection charges if a differential tariff level can be introduced (for example, one that is higher during winter when more garbage is produced).

OPTIONS FOR SERVICE IMPROVEMENTS FOR SOLID WASTE MANAGEMENT

The key area for service improvements of solid waste management would be to increase efficiency in the collection system. At the moment, the frequency of collection is very low: once every month or once every three months per household. The target benchmark is to increase collection frequency to once a week per household.

City Center Ger: Because the bulk of this area will be converted to apartments, the collection system will remain vehicle based. Similar to the current collection system in apartment areas, a transfer station will be installed on the first floor of apartment buildings connected to individual households through a trash chute (see figure 6.3).

If the City Center ger is turned into an apartment area, existing equipment and workers are enough to manage garbage collection and transportation in the area (see table 6.3).

FIGURE 6.3. Solid Waste Collection in Apartment Area

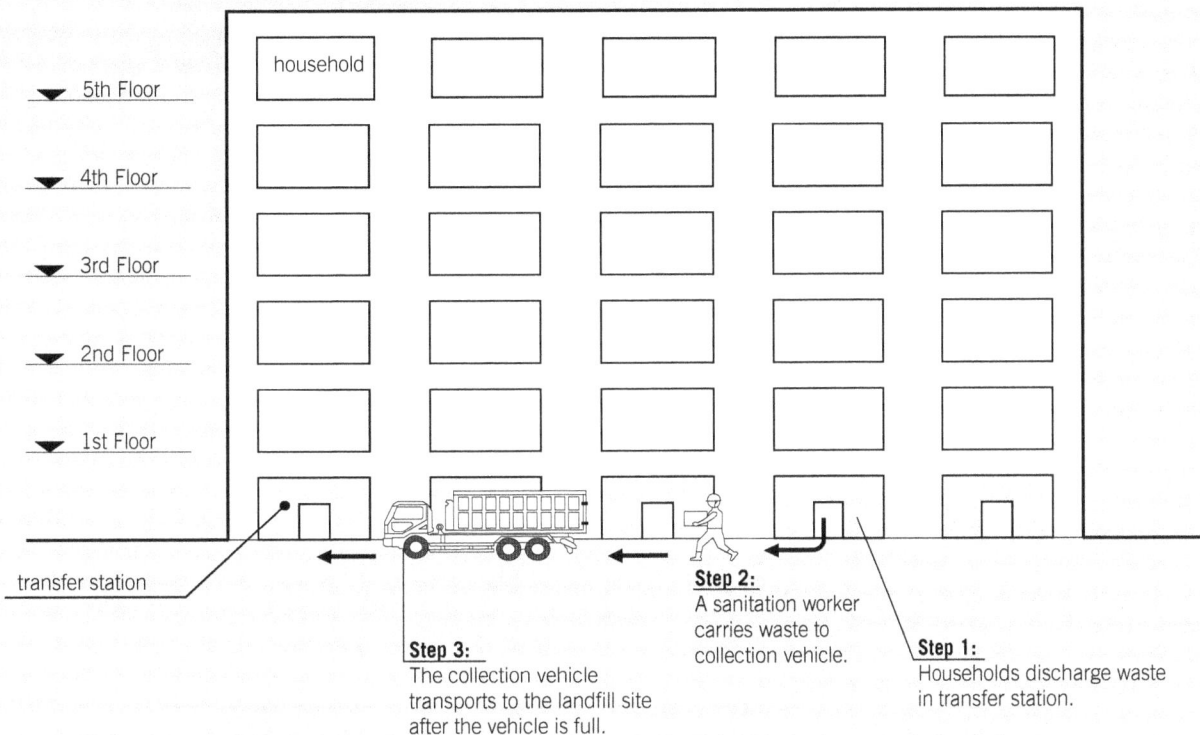

Source: World Bank Task Team estimates 2009.

TABLE 6.3. Procurement Required for Service Improvements in the City Center Ger (Naran), Apartment Area

ITEM		UNIT	CITY CENTER GER
Baseline data	Waste generation	ton/day	12,245
	Times of collection/household	times/week	1
	Round trip distance(landfill)	km	30
Waste collection vehicle	Time spent for collection/transport (LD, TR, UL, RT)	min.	346
		hr.	5.7
	Number of collection vehicles (total)	each	1
	Using existing vehicle	each	1
Workers and driver	Driver	person	1
	Assistant worker	person	2

Source: World Bank Task Team estimates 2009.
Note: LD = Loading; RT = Return; TR = Transfer; UL = Unloading.

Midtier Ger and Fringe Ger: In these two areas, which likely will not be converted to apartment areas in the immediate future, three collection methods can be considered to improve collection

FIGURE 6.4. Solid Waste Collection by Sanitation Workers

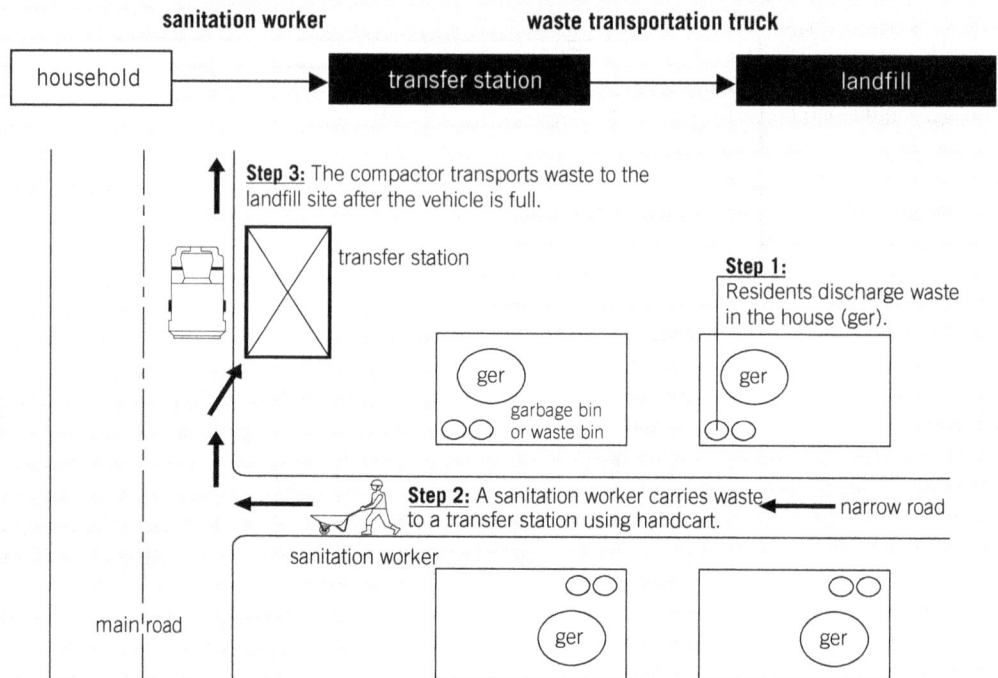

Source: World Bank Task Team estimates 2009.

frequency: collection service by sanitation workers, collection service by residents, and vehicle-based collection. Each method has a different implication for investment and operation costs, which will be discussed in detail.

Option 1: Collection Service by Sanitation Workers. In this case, the waste discharged by each household in a ger is collected by a sanitation worker, who uses a handcart to transport it to a transfer station. Then, the waste is transported from the transfer station to a waste landfill in a high-volume vehicle (see figure 6.4).

Under this option, the required number of sanitation workers and the amount of collection equipment are determined by taking into account collection efficiency, work time, and so forth. In the Midtier ger, six sanitation workers, six handcarts, and two installed transfer stations will be needed. In the Fringe ger, nine sanitation workers, nine handcarts, and three installed transfer stations would be necessary (see table 6.4).

Option 2: Collection Service by Residents. Under this option, the waste is collected by each household in bags. Residents will dispose of the garbage bags themselves in nearby simple transfer facilities or waste containers. The waste collected in containers is then transported to a landfill by a waste transportation vehicle (see figure 6.5). It was estimated that one container is required per 20 households, with the average distance of 100 meters to transfer facilities. Thus, it is estimated that about 84 containers will be needed in the Midtier ger and 125 in the City Center ger. In the Fringe ger, additional vehicles to transport garbage will be needed (see table 6.5).

TABLE 6.4. Procurement Requirement for Service Improvement Option 1

	ITEM	UNIT	MIDTIER GER	FRINGE GER
Baseline data	Population	population	7,979	11,130
	Number of households	household	1,677	2,500
	Population/household	population/household	4.8	4.5
	Waste generation per capita	kg/per capita per day	1.0	1.0
	Waste generation	ton/day	7,979	11,130
	Times of collection/household	times/week	1	1
	Round trip distance (landfill)	km	18	60
Sanitation worker	Collection efficiency of garbage bin	mh/ton	5.8125	5.8125
	Total collection time	hr.	46.4	64.7
	Daily collection time	hr.	8	8
	Number of sanitation workers	person	6	9
	Collection households/sanitation worker	household	280	278
Transfer station	Number of handcarts	each	6	9
	Number of installed transfer stations	each	2	3
Waste collection vehicle	Time spent for collection/transport (1 time) (LD, TR, UL, RT)	min.	92	142
		hr.	1.5	2.4
	Number of collection vehicles (total)	each	1	1
	Using existing vehicle	each	1	1
Number of persons per collection per vehicle	Driver	person	1	1
	Assistant worker	person	2	2

Source: World Bank Task Team estimates 2009.

Option 3: Vehicle-Based Collection. This model is the most similar to the status quo, but it would replace current collection and transportation equipment with a modern collection system. Waste is collected using the door-to-door system and then transported to the landfill. (see figure 6.6) It is estimated that two collection vehicles would be needed in the Midtier ger and three in the Fringe ger (Sharhad). Additional drivers and workers would be needed to operate the new vehicles (see table 6.6).

Each option has its own advantages and disadvantages. Collection by sanitation workers would bring the additional benefits of employment creation by utilizing laborers in ger areas who would otherwise remain unemployed. Collection efficiency will be higher than vehicle-based collection, as waste pickers would go to individual households that are difficult for vehicles to access. This is also the most economical option (See Financial and Economic Implications for details). For the second option of collection by residents using small transfer systems, considerable public education and campaigning on waste disposal would have to accompany its implementation as residents become a part of the collection system. For the option of using the existing vehicle-based collection system, interviews with government officials and residents indicate that this is the most preferred option because it is the system

FIGURE 6.5. Solid Waste Collection by Residents

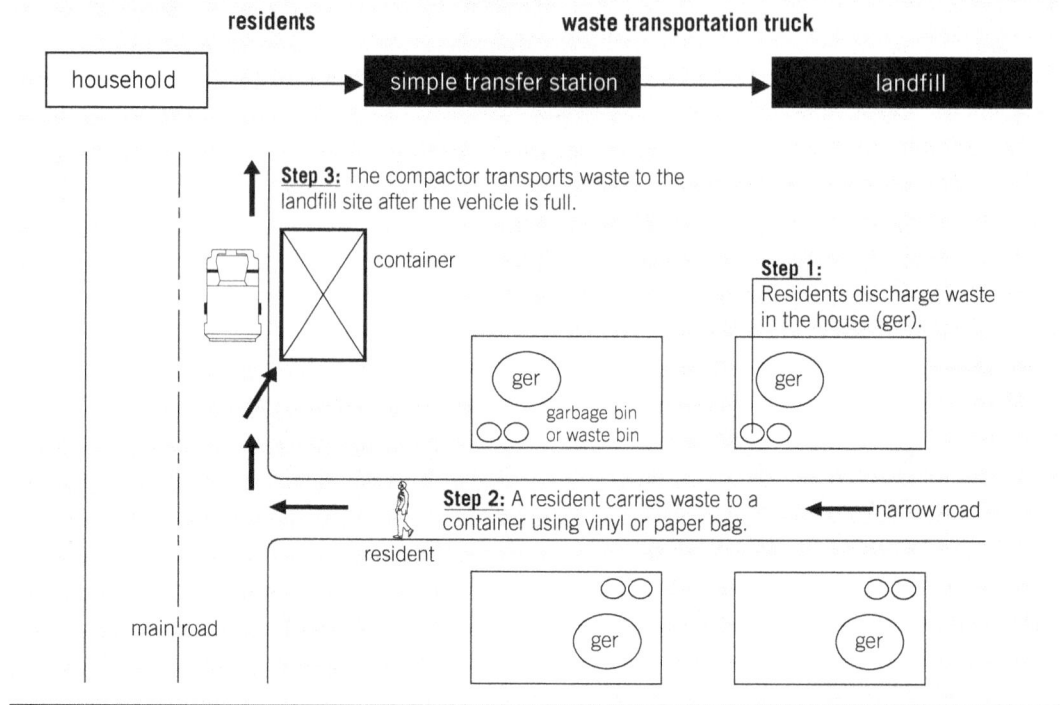

Source: World Bank Task Team estimates 2009.

TABLE 6.5. Procurement Requirement for Service Improvement Option 2

	ITEM	UNIT	MIDTIER GER	FRINGE GER
Baseline data	Population	population	7,979	11,130
	Number of households	household	1,677	2,500
	Population/household	pop/HH	4.8	4.5
	Waste generation per capita	kg/per capita per day	1.0	1.0
	Waste generation	ton/day	7.979	11.130
	Times of collection/household	times/week	1	1
	Round trip distance (landfill)	km	18	60
Simple transfer facilities	Average interval of installation	meter	100	100
	No. of installed facilities (1EA/200household)	each	84	125
Waste collection vehicle	Time spent for collection/transport (LD, TR, UL, RT)	min.	382	607
		hr.	6.4	10.1
	Number of collection vehicle (total)	each	1	2
	Using existing vehicle	each	1	1
	Acquisition of new vehicle	each	—	1
Number of persons per collection per vehicle	Driver	person	1	2
	Assistant worker	person	2	4

Source: World Bank Task Team estimates 2009.

FIGURE 6.6. Solid Waste Collection by Vehicles

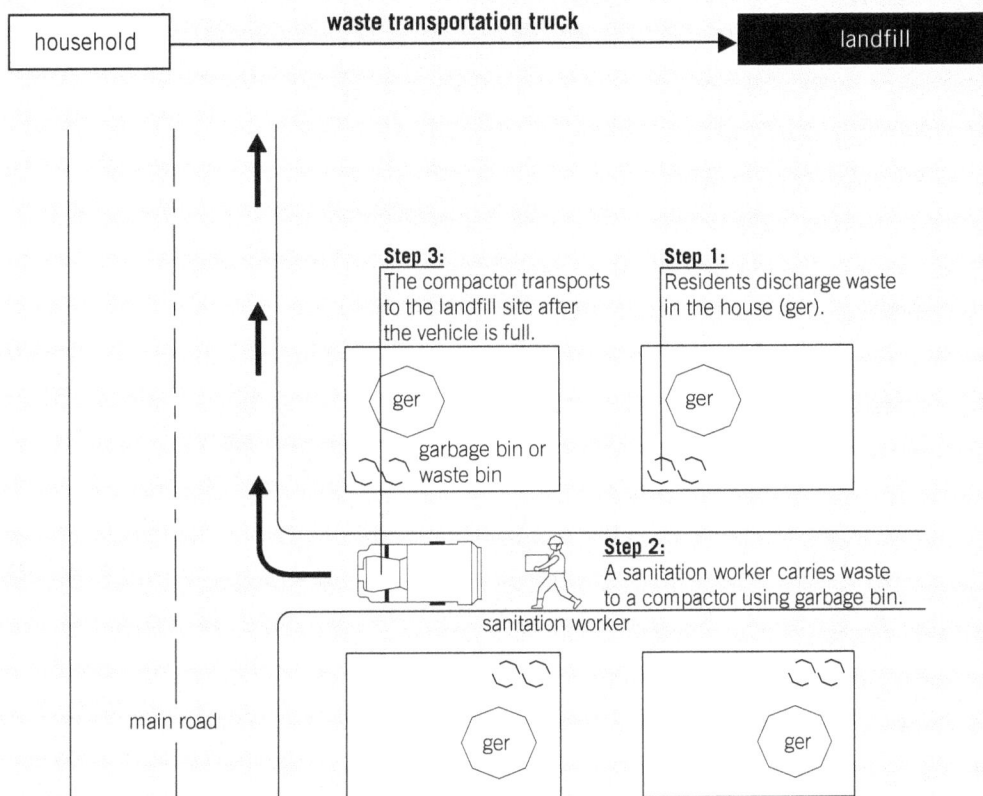

Source: World Bank Task Team estimates 2009.

that they are most familiar with. In all options, a new tariff system will have to be introduced to replace the existing one where residents pay a fee at the time of garbage collection (see table 6.7).

FINANCIAL AND ECONOMIC IMPLICATIONS FOR IMPROVED SOLID WASTE SERVICE

The three options for improving solid waste management bear different financial implications, both in terms of initial investment costs and recurring operating and maintenance costs. As for the investment cost, in case of the City Center ger, which will be turned into an apartment area, existing collection vehicles and equipment are considered sufficient to cover the newly built apartment area. Hence, there should be no additional investment required.

In the Midtier and Fringe gers, however, there is a wide variation among different service options. The lowest cost investment option is collection service done by sanitation workers. The estimated investment cost for this service is about Tg 13.2 million (US$9,400) for the Midtier ger and Tg 19.8 million (US$14,000) for the Fringe ger. In contrast, collection by residents into small transfer systems is the most expensive option, with an estimated cost of about Tg 241 million (US$172,000)

TABLE 6.6. Procurement Requirement for Service Improvement Option 3

	ITEM	UNIT	CITY CENTER GER	MIDTIER GER	FRINGE GER
Baseline data	Population	population	12,245	7,979	11,130
	Number of households	household	3,000	1,677	2,500
	Population/household	pop/HH	4.1	4.8	4.5
	Waste generation per capita	kg/capita.d	1.0	1.0	1.0
	Waste generation	ton/day	12.245	7.979	11.130
	Times of collection/household	times/week	1	1	1
	Round trip distance(landfill)	km	30	18	60
Waste collection vehicle	Time spent for collection/ transport	min.	1,546	872	1,333
	(LD, TR, UL, RT)	hr.	25.8	14.5	22.2
	Number of collection vehicles (total)	each	3	2	3
	Using existing vehicle	each	1	1	1
	Acquisition of new vehicle	each	2	1	2
Number of persons per collection per vehicle	Driver	person	3	2	3
	Assistant worker	person	6	4	6

Source: World Bank Task Team estimates 2009.

and Tg 434 million (US$310,000) in the Midtier and Fringe gers, respectively. Investment costs for vehicle-based collection in the two gers would be Tg 75.6 million (US$54,000) and Tg 152 million (US$108,576), respectively.

As for operation and maintenance, in the City Center ger, about Tg 14.56 million (US$10,400) is the estimated cost per year for labor and vehicle maintenance and operation. In the Midtier and Fringe gers, collection by residents into small transfer systems would entail about one-half of the operation and maintenance cost of the other two options. Using sanitation workers would cost about Tg 16.5 million (US$11,800) and Tg 16.5 million (US$25,500) in the Midtier and Fringe gers, respectively. The most expensive option, vehicle-based collection, would require Tg 16.1 million (US$11,500) and Tg 58.8 million (US$42,000) per year in the two gers, respectively.

From a service provider's perspective, the first option—a system of collection by sanitation workers—seems the most cost-effective, considering the initial required investment and the annual operation and maintenance costs (see table 6.8).

All of the proposed options will increase both the frequency of collection and the volume of collected solid waste, thereby putting additional pressure on the city landfill. Operating costs for the landfill, currently around Tg 1.54 billion (US$1.1 million) annually, will increase as the frequency of delivery increases. With the likely boost in volume, the estimated 20-year life of the landfill may be shortened slightly. The costs of an additional landfill site are estimated at Tg 52.36 billion (US$37.4 million) for a 7.5 million m³ landfill.

The current collection tariff level is set by the municipal council at Tg 2,500 per household (about US$1.79 per month) in ger areas, higher than the tariff for apartment residents at Tg 2,000 (US$1.43). In three ger areas, tariffs range from Tg 1,500 to Tg 3,000 (US$1.07 to US$2.14). This relatively high level of tariff is mostly due to the low collection rate and to the lack of government subsidy. For an estimate of the financial burden for households, the tariff level was computed to cover just operation and maintenance costs, not investment or depreciation. The resulting tariff varies considerably across ger areas, depending on service options. Households in the Midtier ger are expected to pay at least Tg 410 to Tg 830 (US$0.29 to US$0.59) per month. Those in the Fringe ger pay from Tg 1,320 to Tg 1,960 (US$0.94 to US$1.40), and those in the City Center ger pay Tg 410 (US$0.29) for new apartment areas (see table 6.9).

TABLE 6.7. Comparison of Different Options for Service Improvement

CLASSIFICATION	ADVANTAGES	CHALLENGES
Option 1 Collection service by sanitation worker	• To create jobs by using personnel in gers, areas with high unemployment, as sanitation workers • To solve the issue of waste stagnancy in each home by increasing collection frequency • To increase collection and transportation efficiency compared to the current collection system by direct door-to-door collection system • To increase the collection rate of recyclable materials by operating the transfer station • To have the most economical program	• A new tariff system needs to be introduced replacing current one, which levies tariff at the time of collection. • Land should be acquired to install a transfer station. • The transfer station poses the risk of fire. • Local residents may complain about dust, stench, and noise from the transfer station.
Option 2 Collection service by residents	• To improve the awareness of residents because they are part of collection system. • To reduce waste collection and transport cost • To reduce the amount of stagnant waste in the house, because the resident personally disposes waste to the transfer station	• A new tariff system needs to be introduced replacing the current one, which levies tariff at the time of collection. • It is necessary to encourage residents to participate voluntarily, through publicity and education campaigns. • Land should be acquired to install a transfer station with the consent of local residents. • Local residents may complain about dust, stench, and noise from the transfer station.
Option 3 Collection service by vehicle	• The most familiar system, which simply supplements the collection equipment of the current collection system • System most preferred by residents and public officials	• Because the collection interval is too long, it must improve the collection vehicles and collection containers. • The collection rate may remain very low. • Current tariff system is not financially viable, and a new tariff system needs to be adopted.

Source: World Bank Task Team estimates 2009.

TABLE 6.8. Initial Investment Cost and Operation Cost to Improve Waste Collection Service

	ITEM		UNIT	CITY CENTER GER	MIDTIER GER	FRINGE GER
Option 1 (sanitation workers/ handcarts)	Initial investment	Buying handcart	each	—	6	9
			million Tg (unit)	—	0.73	0.73
			million Tg (total)	—	4.38	6.58
		Installing T/S	million Tg	—	8.82	13.23
		Total cost	**million Tg**	—	**13.20**	**19.81**
	Operation	Labor cost	million Tg/year	—	15.22	29.23
		Operating C/V	million Tg/year	—	1.37	6.41
		Total cost	**million Tg/year**	—	**16.59**	**35.65**
Option 2 (small transfer stations)	Initial investment	Installing STF	each	—	84	125
			million Tg (unit)	—	2.87	2.87
			million Tg (total)	—	240.96	358.58
		Buying C/V	each	—	—	1
			million Tg (unit)	—	—	76.00
			million Tg (total)	—	—	76.00
		Total cost	**million Tg**	—	**240.96**	**434.58**
	Operation	Labor cost	million Tg/year	—	6.75	33.06
		Operating C/V	million Tg/year	—	1.37	6.41
		Total cost	**million Tg/year**	—	**8.12**	**39.48**
Option 3 (improved status quo)	Initial investment	Buying C/V	each	2	1	2
			million Tg (unit)	76.00	76.00	76.00
			million Tg (total)	152.01	76.00	152.01
		Total cost	**million Tg**	**152.01**	**76.00**	**152.01**
	Operation	Labor cost	million Tg/year	32.81	13.51	49.59
		Operating C/V	million Tg/year	7.09	2.66	9.12
		Total cost	**million Tg/year**	**39.90**	**16.17**	**58.71**

Source: World Bank Task Team estimates 2009.
Note: C/V = Collection Vehicle; STF = Small Transfer Station; T/S = Transfer Station.

TABLE 6.9. Expected Tariff Level for Solid Waste Management

HOUSEHOLD	COSTS	CITY CENTER GER	MIDTIER GER	FRINGE GER
		3,000	1,677	2,500
Current tariff (Tg)		2,996	1,498	2,492
Option 1: Sanitation workers	Annual O&M cost (million Tg/year)		16.59	35.65
	Cost per household (Tg/month)		**826**	**1,190**
Option 2: Small transfer systems	Annual O&M cost (million Tg/year)		8.12	39.48
	Cost per household (Tg/month)		**406**	**1,316**
Option 3: Improved status quo	Annual O&M cost (million Tg/year)	14.54	16.17	58.71
	Cost per household (Tg/month)	**406**	**112,798**	**1,960**

Source: World Bank Task Team estimates 2009.
Note: O&M = operations and maintenance.

7 Heating

Ulaanbaatar (UB) is one of the coldest capitals in the world, making reliable and affordable heating vital for sustainable livelihood and development. The heating season lasts around eight months, from mid-September until mid-May. The fuel for all the heating options in Mongolia is based on indigenous coal or wood. The use of raw coal in heat-only boilers (HOB) and household stoves is considered one of the main causes of worsening air quality in UB. According to a recent air pollution assessment in UB, the ground-level air pollution, measured in terms of particulate matter (PM10), during winter is estimated to be between three and six times higher than the levels recommended in Europe and North America, and 10 to 20 times higher than the World Health Organization–recommended standards. It has been well established that airborne particulate matter is a critical pollutant responsible for negative health outcomes, such as respiratory illnesses, premature death, and restricted activity days. This factor implies a severe effect on both human health costs and economic costs to the society. The Municipality of Ulaanbaatar (MUB) is keen to ban the use of raw coal and to develop and promote the use of cleaner fuels, such as semicoke briquettes. In fact, in recent years the UB government has spent several billion tugriks in subsidies to promote the use of cleaner briquettes.

According to the above context, this chapter describes the current situation of heating systems in the three ger areas, brings forward possible service improvement options, and estimates associated costs and benefits.

CURRENT STATUS OF HEATING IN GER AREAS

In general, four different types of existing heating systems are used in Mongolia: (a) centralized (or district) heating systems, (b) small-district heating systems for groups of buildings (heat-only boilers, or HOB, or boiler houses), (c) individual heating systems (water heaters), and (d) household stoves.

Centralized (or district) heating offers a number of benefits over decentralized heating options in areas of high heat-load density. One of the key advantages of centralized heating is an increased use of combined heat and power (CHP) production, which results in increased efficiency of the use of the primary energy (coal in the case of Mongolia) and a positive effect on the ambient air quality. There are significant economic benefits of centralized (or district heating), such as low production costs compared to any other types of individual boilers, and fuel savings (and related environmental impacts), because of economies of scale and high heat-load density. CHP generation provides up to 30 percent fuel savings compared to those of HOB. Therefore, centralized (or district) heating is more efficient in terms of cost of service and environmental friendliness. This efficiency is widely understood: in Germany, there is even legislation that subsidizes CHP generation.

District heating can be efficient and suitable for densely populated urban areas with a high heat-load density per km of network. The heat density in ger areas is very low, however, and can be as much as 40–50 times lower than in apartment complexes. Because of the unplanned development of ger areas, it is technically almost impossible to provide district heating. Even if it were technically feasible to connect those ger areas, without proper heat insulation and energy efficiency measures on the demand side, it would be a waste of resources. Traditional gers and detached houses in ger areas are not efficient in terms of heat insulation. On average, gers lose about 4–5 times and houses lose about 2–3 times as much heat as the national standards for heat insulation.

In Mongolia, the electricity sector is closely linked to the heat sector because most heat supplied in the central energy system (CES) is produced from five CHP plants in Ulaanbaatar, Darkhan, and Erdenet. Though cogeneration of heat and power provides the most efficient energy usage, significant improvements are required to reduce energy losses in the existing heat distribution system, to meter properly, and to regulate heat consumption on the demand side.

Coal-fired water heaters can heat up to 100–500 m^3 space and are installed in the boiler houses. The number of those stoves has increased significantly since the early 1990s with the transition to the market economy system and the establishment of numerous small businesses and services. Coal-fired water heaters have low capacity and are used mostly in ger areas by small businesses, shops, services, and so forth. All those heaters use raw coal, contributing to UB city air pollution. A recent study revealed that 1,005 coal-fired water heaters in six districts in UB use about 11,900 tons of raw coal per heating season. In terms of capacity, there are 514 (51.1 percent) water heaters with a capacity of 1–10 kW, 226 (22.5 percent) with a capacity of 10–20 kW, 192 (19.1 percent) with a capacity of 20–50 kW, 40 (4 percent) with a capacity of 50–90 kW, and 33 (3.3 percent) with a capacity of 90–120 kW. All of these water heaters are designed for heating only one structure that usually has two or three rooms.

Heat-only boilers (HOB) include boilers that can produce 0.2–1.0 Gcal/hour (250–1,000 kW) and are used mostly to heat one or several schools, kindergartens, and hospitals. There are 166 boilers of 24 different types in 89 boiler houses in UB. In the 2007–08 heating season, their total coal consumption was 66,643 tons. In terms of capacity, there are 32 (35.6 percent) boiler houses with a capacity of 0–0.2 Gcal/h, 40 (44.9 percent) with a capacity of 0.2–0.6 Gcal/h, 10 (11.2 percent) with a capacity of 0.6–1.0 Gcal/h, and 7 boiler houses with a capacity of more than 90–120 kW.

Heating stoves are used in a variety of ways. Stoves can be used directly for space heating, or a heating wall is attached to the stove for better heat distribution. Some stoves have a hot water distribution system and radiators to heat the house; this system is commonly known in Mongolia as a small, low-pressure boiler. Recently, different modifications of improved stoves have been developed to reduce fuel consumption and CO_2 emissions. In the three targeted ger areas, almost all households, except some apartments-dwellers in the City Center ger (Naran), use traditional stoves for heating.

City Center Ger (Naran), 11th khoroo, Bayangol District: Three different types of heating are now represented in this area: small business water heaters, households with individual stoves, and apartment buildings and public organizations connected to the district heating system (see table 7.1).

For households using individual stoves, the heat loss is considerably higher—two or three times the national standards for heat insulation. Average heat load for private houses is about 5.9 kW and for

TABLE 7.1. Current Status of Heating Supply in Selected Khoroos

| KHOROO | TOTAL HOUSEHOLDS | TYPES OF HEATING | | | |
		DISTRICT HEATING	HEAT-ONLY BOILER (HOB)	WATER HEATERS	STOVES
Bayangol district, 11th khoroo	2,970	130 households, 6 organizations, and 10 apartment buildings		30 small businesses	2,840
Songino Khairkhan district, 8th khoroo, Bayankhoshuu ger area	1,677	N/A	HOB at school #67, 15 small businesses, and 20 private houses	20 small businesses	1,677
Bayanzürkh district, 9th khoroo, Sharhad ger area	2,567	N/A	N/A	43 small businesses	2,567

gers is about 4.8 kW. The total current heat load for houses and gers is 16.8 MW, and these households use 11,930 tons of coal and 2,550 tons of firewood. Annual spending on fuel amounts to about Tg 1 billion (US$714,000).[1]

Approximately 30 small businesses, mainly service companies, use their own heaters. Those boilers generate hot water for heating. There is also one bathhouse with four individial cabins and six common showers connected to the centralized heat networks. The community requested that an additional two or three bathhouses be built in the near future. Their total design heat loads are 1,157.5 kW.

In addition, one boiler house in this khoroo supplies heat to 46th Secondary School (for 2,000 students) and the khoroo's administrative building. The 46th Secondary School was originally connected to the central heating system, but because of limited heating capacity, it was disconnected from the system in 1996; since then, the school has operated its own boiler house. The heat load of the school is 400 kW.

Midtier Ger (Bayankhoshuu), 8th Khoroo, Songino Khairkhan District: Broadly, there are three types of heating systems in the ger area: (a) larger consumers, such as schools and kindergartens connected to boiler houses, (b) small businesses and services with their own heaters, and (c) individual houses or gers with stoves.

The 67th Secondary School and 117th Kindergarten are connected to and receive heating from the boiler house operated by the ANU Service Company. The design heat load is 920 kW, heating is billed per cubic meter of space, and the heating charge is Tg 462 per cubic meter. Also, approximately 20 small businesses and services have their own heaters. The total design heat load is 1,378 kW. Most of the small businesses are located at Bayankhoshuu's bus station and use inefficient stoves from local and Chinese manufacturers.

Similar to Naran, most households that use stoves suffer from high heat loss—two or three times the standard rate. The average heat load for private houses is about 5.9 kW and for gers is about 4.8 kW. The total current heat load for houses and gers is 13.7 MW; those households use 7,044 tons of coal and 1,510 tons of firewood annually, spending about Tg 593.8 million (about US$424,000) for heating and other purposes.[2] One bathhouse in this khoroo near the family hospital titled "Eeltei" is not working, and the community has requested at least two or three new bathhouses.

Fringe Ger (Sharhad), 9th Khoroo, Bayanzürkh District: Similar to the other two, the following heating systems are in this khoroo: (a) larger consumers, such as schools and kindergartens connected to boiler houses; (b) small businesses and services with their own heaters; and (c) individual houses or gers with stoves.

Within this khoroo is the 79th Elementary School with 1,160 pupils, the 3rd Kindergarten with 190 children, as well as the National Centre of Psychological Health (Psychoneurological Hospital). The kindergarten and school have their own boiler houses. The Psychoneurological Hospital boiler house has two sections: heating and hot water supply. Their total design heat loads are 2760 kW. The commercial service facilities within this khoroo are located close to each other near the Sharhad bus terminal. Also near the bus terminal is an old boiler house building, which stopped functioning because it lacked maintenance. It would be possible to use this building and site for a modern boiler house.

Of 2,567 households in this khoroo, about 70 percent have wall stoves. Heat loss for almost all houses is 2–3 times the standard rate. The households consume more than 10,000 tons of coal per year and another 2,300 tons of wood for heating. The wholesale price of one ton of coal is about Tg 65,000 (US$46), and its retail price is about Tg 130,000 (US$93). The wholesale price of one ton of wood is about Tg 90,000 (US$64), which amounts to Tg 200,000 (US$143) in retail price. The Khuslen service center has one bath house with 10 common showers. Price of service is Tg 1,600 (US$1.14) per person. The community requested two or three bath houses in the near future.

OPTIONS FOR SERVICE IMPROVEMENTS AND FINANCIAL IMPLICATIONS

City Center Ger (Naran), 11th Khoroo, Bayangol District: This area will be connected to district heating given its proximity to the district heating network, but the following factors need to be taken into account:

For newly developed apartment complexes. There is 6.0 MW of heating capacity at the 728th substation, which is already planned to be connected to buildings in neighboring khoroos. The construction of some of the buildings has already started, with plans to build a heating substation with a capacity of 10 MW capacity on the east side of the Maternal and Children's Hospital. This substation will supply the heating to a new apartment complex, which is planned to be built by 2010. The complex will have 900 apartment units; some of those will serve about 120 households that have lived in the area and will receive apartments in exchange for their land. The cost to provide a centralized heating system in the apartment area is around Tg 612 million (US$437,400), including the installation of a new heat substation for around Tg 210 million (US$150,000) and a heat pipe network for Tg 402 million (US$287,400), or around Tg 680,400 (US$486) per connection of each apartment unit (see table 7.2).

TABLE 7.2. Total Investment Costs of Installing a New Heat Substation with Heat Network

LOCATION AND PROPOSED INVESTMENTS	UNIT	UNIT COST	VOLUME	TOTAL US$
Installation of a new heat substation in the east side of the Maternal and Children's Hospital	MW	15,000/MW	10.0	$150,000
Installation of a new heat pipeline from the main line to the new heat substation	2 x D200 mm	310 US$/m	150 m	$46,500
Installation of a new heat pipe from the new heat substation to apartments	2 x D250 mm	330 US$/m	730 m	$240,900
Total				$437,400

Source: World Bank Task Team estimates 2009.

The cost of connecting existing small businesses to a district heating network is high, even if district heating capacity is available. There is a limited technical possibility of connecting about 20 small private businesses near 46th Secondary School to district heating. The total connection cost would be Tg 170,000 (US$121) or about Tg 8,500 (US$6) per connection. A recent survey conducted among small businesses shows that they all are interested in being connected to district heating.

The cost of connecting existing detached houses and gers to district heating is also high. The cost per individual connection will be about Tg 3.4 million (US$2,415), including Tg 476,000 (US$340) for construction of the main heating pipeline, Tg 1.2 million (US$850) for construction of the boiler, and Tg 1.8 million (US$1,250) for installation of the indoor heating and water system. The total cost of connecting to the district heating network will be around Tg 9.2 billion (US$6.6 million) for a heat network of 4.6 km and a boiler house with a capacity of 16.0 MW.

For the district to connect new apartment complexes to district heating, the capacity of existing district heating would have to be enhanced. Ulaanbaatar district heating networks have already reached maximum heating capacity. Unless the new heating sources are in place, it is technically not feasible to allow new connections. The total available heating capacity from the three power plants in UB is 1,585 Gcal/h, and the applications for new connections would add 283 Gcal/h, creating a deficit of 1,37.4 Gcal/h if connected. Starting in 2010, the UB city will not be able to make any new connections to district heating because of heat supply shortages. In addition, obsolete heating pipelines and networks require significant rehabilitation measures, without which the UB district heating network cannot ensure reliable heat supply. The Ministry of Mineral Resources and Energy is in the process of tendering bidders to develop Power Plant #5, which is planned in the eastern part of the city, with heat capacity around 700 Gcal/h.

Midtier Ger (Bayankhoshuu), 8th Khoroo, Songino Khairkhan District: Two options for service improvements are expanding the capacity of local HOB and connecting them to the local heating network, or connecting to the district heating system.

Expansion of capacity at the existing boiler house at 67th School and connection of nearby users. This expansion would increase the heating capacity of ANU Service Co. Ltd's boiler at 67th Secondary School

TABLE 7.3. Total Investment Cost of Installing a New Boiler House and Heat Network

LOCATION AND PROPOSED INVESTMENTS	UNIT	UNIT COST (US$)	VOLUME	TOTAL COST (US$)
Installation of a new boiler house in the ger area	kW	$144.1 /kW	5,9*2720 = 16050.0 kw	2,312,800
Installation of a heat network from a new boiler house	2 x D250 mm	$330.0 /m	45.0 m	14,850
	2 x D180 mm	$300.0 /m	545.0 m	163,500
	2 x D150 mm	$260.0 /m	400.0 m	104,000
	2 x D125 mm	$220.0 /m	700.0 m	154,000
	2 x D100 mm	$150.8 /m	1,100.0 m	165,880
	2 x D70 mm	$145.8 /m	866.4 m	126,320
	2 x D50 mm	$135.0 /m	950.0 m	128,250
	Total		4,606.0 m	856,600
Installation of indoor heating and water system in private houses		$1,250 /one house	2,720.0 m	3,400,000
Total				6,569,400

Source: World Bank Task Team estimates 2009.

from 1,170 to 1,470 kW and would connect to its network all potential customers near the Bayankhoshuu bus terminal. Total heat load of customers near the bus terminal is 300 kW, with 200 kW for customers located in the khoroo. The capacity of the heating boilers located in 67th Secondary School could be increased to allow connections to the small service buildings close to Bayankhoshuu's former bus terminal. Approximately 20 services companies have their own heaters, which generate hot water for heating. Technical data of heat consumers and boilers are shown in table 7.3. Their total design heat loads are 1,378.0 kW.

The capital investment to improve the heating capacity of this boiler by 300 kW is Tg 121.8 million (US$87,000), including Tg 58.8 million (US$42,000) for upgrading boiler capacity and Tg 63 million (US$45,000) for constructing new heating pipelines. The coal price is Tg 84,000 (US$60) per ton. After improvements to the boiler, the price for one Gcal heating will be Tg 66,500 (US$47.5). This price is less than the current expense of heating small buildings. The owners of these services companies all accept this option. Total investment costs of installing new boilers and heating network are shown in table 7.4.

Expansion of capacity at existing boiler house at 67th School and the connection of nearby users. Customers located near Bayankhoshuu's bus terminal can be connected to the heating network of Talst Echim

TABLE 7.4. Total Investment Cost of Installing New Boilers and a Heat Network

LOCATION AND PROPOSED INVESTMENTS	UNIT	UNIT COST	VOLUME	TOTAL COST (US$)
Installation of a new boiler at the boiler house at 67th School	kW	140 $/kW	300.0	**42,000**
Installation of a heat pipe at the boiler house at 67th School	2 x D100 mm	150.8 $/m	105.0 m	15,834
	2 x D 80 mm	145.8 $/m	200.0 m	29,166
				45,000
Total				87,000

Source: World Bank Task Team estimates 2009.

TABLE 7.5. Total Investment Cost of Installing of Improved Boilers and a Heat Network

LOCATION AND PROPOSED INVESTMENTS	UNIT	UNIT COST (US$)	VOLUME	TOTAL COST (US$)
Replacement of three BZIU-100 at the boiler house at 67th School	kW	$140 /kW	1,100	**154,000**
Installation of a heat pipe at the boiler house at 76th School	2 x D125 mm	$220.0 /m	387.0 m	85,150
	2 x D100 mm	$150.8 /m	390.0 m	58,812
	2 x D 80 mm	$145.8 /m	110.0 m	16,038
	Total			**160,000**
Total				314,000

Source: World Bank Task Team estimates 2009.

Co., Ltd., and its boiler house at the 67th Secondary School. There are three BZIU-100 and one ECO-500 boilers in the boiler houses, with a capacity of 2,600 kW. Because the BZIU-100 units are quite inefficient, they should be changed to modern boilers of the same capacity and high efficiency. The actual heat load is 980 kW (0.84 Gcal/hour), and the designed heat load for new customers from the Fringe ger is 500kW (15 commercial services and about 20 private houses) and from the Midtier ger is 100 kW.

The capital investment for renewing the boiler in Bayankhoshuu's new bus terminal with a high-efficiency version is Tg 439.6 million (US$314,000), including Tg 215.6 million (US$154,000) for renewal and Tg 224 million (US$160,000) for construction of new heating pipelines. The coal price is Tg 84,000 (US$60) per ton, and the fuel-cost ratio of total operating and maintenance costs for Ulaanbaatar city is 0.6. After the improvement of the boilers, the price for one Gcal heating is expected to be around Tg 66,500 (US$47.50). This cost is less than the current heating expense of small buildings. The total investment costs of installing new boilers and heating network are shown in table 7.5. After implementing those options, the coal consumption is likely to be reduced by 922 tons annually, and greenhouse gas (GHG) emissions will be reduced by 1,250 tons annually.

Cost of connecting existing houses to the district heating. About Tg 5.67 billion (US$4.05 million) would be required to connect these households to the centralized heating system (heat network of 2,840 meters and boiler house with a capacity of 9,894.0 kW) (see table 7.6). The investment amount per household is Tg 3.4 million (US$2,415), including Tg 441,000 (US$315) for constructing heating main lines, Tg 1,190,000 (US$850) for boiler construction, and Tg 1,750,000 (US$1,250) for installation of an indoor heating and water system. The annual heating cost for households will be 2.7 times higher than the conventional system, or Tg 931,000 (US$665) per year. Household income could not cover these expenses without a significant government subsidy, which is unrealistic at this point.

A more realistic and effective option would be to improve building insulation. The insulation cost for a house of 36 m² is Tg 266,000 (US$190). Once insulation is complete, the consumption of coal can be reduced by 2.2 times, to around two tons per heating season. In addition, it is likely that fuel expenses will be reduced by Tg 260,000 (US$185.71) and GHG emissions reduced to 2.7 tons per season.

TABLE 7.6. Total Investment Cost of Installing a New Boiler House and Heat Network

LOCATION	PROPOSED IMPROVEMENT	UNIT	UNIT COST (US$)	VOLUME	TOTAL COST (US$)
Boiler house in ger area	Installation of a new boiler house	kW	144.1 /kW	5,9*1,192 = 9,894.0 kw	1,425,725
Heat network from a new boiler house	Heat pipes installation	2 x D250 mm	330 /m	52.6 m	**17,360**
		2 x D180 mm	300 /m	311.0 m	**93,300**
		2 x D150 mm	260 /m	236.0 m	**61,360**
		2 x D125 mm	220 /m	440.0 m	**96,800**
		2 x D100 mm	151 /m	670.0 m	**101,036**
		2 x D70 mm	146 /m	540.0 m	**78,732**
		2 x D50 mm	135 /m	590.0 m	**79,650**
		Total		**2,840.0 m**	528,240
Ger or private houses	installation of an indoor heating and water system		1,250 /for one house	1,677.0	2,096,250
Total					**4,050,000**

Source: World Bank Task Team estimates 2009.

Residents expressed a strong interest in having hot water and showers in their houses or at a nearby area. In the middle of the ger, two bathhouses with individual heaters can be built. The investment cost of installing one bathhouse, capable of serving 100 persons daily (35,000 annually), is Tg 140 million (US$100,000). If the service fee is Tg 1,250 (US$0.89) per person, the capital investment will be recovered in three years after the installation.

Fringe Ger (Sharhad), 9th Khoroo, Bayanzürkh District: Options available to improve heat supply include (a) installation at the bus terminal of a new, high-efficiency boiler house larger than 1.6 MW; (b) installation of a new heating network from a new boiler house; (c) replacement of three old boilers (type BZIU-100) at Psychoneurological Hospital with new, high-efficiency boilers; and (d) installation of two new bathhouses in the center of the ger area.

Most of the 43 small service buildings are near the Sharhad bus terminal. There is no boiler house in that area. It is possible to build a new boiler with 1.6 MW capacity to connect the service buildings to the centralized heating system. The capital investment for this boiler is estimated to be Tg 604.8 million (US$432,000), including Tg 420 million (US$300,000) for improvements to the building and installation of the new boiler, and Tg 184.8 million (US$132,000) for the construction of new heating pipelines (see table 7.7). The coal price is Tg 84,000 (US$60) per ton. The fuel-cost ratio of total operating and maintenance costs for Ulaanbaatar city is 0.6.

After the boiler is installed, the price for one Gcal heating will be Tg 66,500 (US$47.50). This price will be affordable to the small store owners. The total investment costs of installing new boilers and heating network are shown in table 7.7. If this option is implemented, the coal consumption will be reduced by 1,000 tons, and GHG emission will be reduced by 1,360 tons annually.

Replacing three old boilers (type BZIU-100) at the Psychoneurological Hospital's boiler house with new high-efficiency boilers will cost an estimated Tg 372.4 million (US$266,000). When

TABLE 7.7. Total Investment Cost of Installing New Boilers and a Heating Network

LOCATION	PROPOSED IMPROVEMENT	UNIT	UNIT COST (US$)	VOLUME	TOTAL (US$)
Sharhad bus terminal	Installation of a new boiler house with higher efficiency	kW	140/kW	1600.0	240,000
Sharhad bus terminal	Installation of a new heat pipeline	2 x D125 mm 2 x D100 mm 2 x D80 mm	220.0 /m 150.8 /m 145.8 /m	230.0 284.5 264.0	50,600 42,910 38,490 **132,000**

Source: World Bank Task Team estimates 2009.

high-efficiency boilers are run, the coal consumption will be reduced by 1,245 tons, and the heating expenses will be reduced by Tg 104.6 million (US$74,700) annually. The capital investment will be recovered in three to four years because of reduced coal consumption. Total investment costs of installing new boilers are shown in table 7.8.

Connecting households to the centralized heating system will need an estimated Tg 8.7 billion (US$6.2 million) for the heat network of 4,320 meters and boiler house with a capacity of 15,145.0 kW. The investment amount per household would be Tg 34 million (US$2,412), including Tg 436,800 (US$312) for the heat network, Tg 1.2 million (US$850) for the boiler, and Tg 1.8 million (US$1,250) for installation of the indoor heating and water system (see table 7.9). Similar to the Midtier ger scenario, this option is not financially viable, and a better option would be to improve building insulation.

The following conclusions can be drawn from this analysis:

☐ Integrating ger areas into the district heating system is costly even in the City Center ger, where the central networks are already distributed nearby. The estimated cost per connection for a limited number of small businesses to the existing centralized heating system will be around Tg 1.8 million (US$8,500), and the cost per connection of individual households is around Tg 3.4 million (US$2,415). Connection to the district heating system does not make much sense without improving the heating insulation of existing houses and small structures. In addition to scattered locations and low heat density, the existing individual houses and homes lose as much as two to three times more heat compared to national heat insulation standards.

☐ For the Midtier and Fringe gers, expanding or rehabilitating onsite boilers, improving housing insulation and existing stoves, and providing public bathhouses seem to be more economical options.

TABLE 7.8. Total Investment Cost of Installing New Boilers

LOCATION	PROPOSED IMPROVEMENT	UNIT	UNIT COST	VOLUME	TOTAL (US$)
Psychoneurological Hospital's boiler house	Replacement of old boilers	kW	US$140 /kW	1,900	**266,000**

Source: World Bank Task Team estimates 2009.
Note: For this table, US$1 = Tg 1,450.

TABLE 7.9. Total Investment Cost of Installing New Boiler House and Heat Network

LOCATION	PROPOSED IMPROVEMENT	UNIT	UNIT COST	VOLUME	TOTAL COST (US$)
Boiler house in ger area	Installation of new boiler house	kW	144.1 $/kW	5,9*2567 = 15145.0 kw	2,182,440
Heat network from new boiler house	Heat pipes installation	2 x D250 mm	330.0 $/m	40.0 m	13,200
		2 x D180 mm	300.0 $/m	515.0 m	154,500
		2 x D150 mm	260.0$/m	340.0 m	88,400
		2 x D125 mm	220.0 $/m	670.0 m	147,400
		2 x D100 mm	150.8 $/m	1030.0 m	155,325
		2 x D70 mm	145.8 $/m	825.0 m	120,285
		2 x D50 mm	135.0 $/m	900.0 m	121,500
		Total		**4,320.0 m**	**800,610**
Ger or private houses	Installation of indoor heating and water system		1,250.0 $ for one house	2,567.0	3,208,750
Total					**6,191,800**

Source: World Bank Task Team estimates 2009.

☐ The ger residents will have no choice but to continue using stoves because alternative improvements such as district heating or local boilers are too expensive. Given this reality, technical options for energy-efficient stoves, alternative fuels, and housing insulation would have to be further developed.

☐ Ger residents bear a high financial burden of heating costs. According to a recent Bank survey,[3] the estimated total expenditure per household during the heating season is Tg 174,767 (US$125) for raw coal and Tg 84,853 (US$61) for firewood. More important, the same survey reveals that lower income households in the ger districts spend a significant amount of money to heat their gers or homes. The financial burden is extremely high for households in the bottom fifth income quintile; they spend as much as 40 percent of their monthly winter income on heating fuels, compared to similar expenditures of only 9 percent by households in the top income quintile.

8 Electricity

OVERVIEW OF CURRENT STATUS OF ELECTRICITY

Ulaanbaatar (UB) city is growing rapidly, both as the ger areas swell as a result of the influx of migrants from rural areas, and with the rapid construction of the urban center and housing developments. The World Bank–financed Energy Sector Project (ESP) has produced good results in reducing technical and nontechnical losses in ger areas in UB, improving revenue collection, and in commercializing the distribution business of the Ulaanbaatar Electricity Distribution Network Company (UBEDN). The project has successfully lowered technical and nontechnical losses from an average of 31 percent to 20 percent in UB ger areas. Billing and revenue collection have improved dramatically (bill collection days have been reduced from 98 to 57 days in UB).

Despite these improvements, the city's electricity service still faces significant challenges. Nearly 70 percent of underground cables have exceeded their technical life spans, and some 425 cable faults are reported annually. Half of the 75 main substation transformers have been in service for more than 25 years; nine have been in use for more than 40 years. Because of the global financial crisis and the sharp drop in commodity prices for Mongolia's major export commodities, the risk of compounding the economic crisis if the electricity system fails is very high.

Mongolia's current total installed electricity capacity is 878.4 MW. The recently updated Energy Sector Master Plan forecasted that power demand is expected to increase at an annual rate of 2.9 percent between 2001 and 2020. However, the actual average power demand growth for the past three years average was 5 percent. Because of reduced reliability and insufficient capacity of the distribution network, the UBEDN has to stop new connections (almost 150 connections for new buildings in 43 locations). The gsovernment had announced a bid to construct a new combined heat and power (CHP) plant #5 in UB, but because of the lack of proper planning and due diligence process, the tender has been cancelled. The government has requested additional financing from the ongoing ESP for crucial investments in UB's distribution and transmission networks. Immediate financing is needed to meet the increasing demands for expansion and rehabilitation of the distribution and transmission networks in Mongolia's Central Region, estimated to be around US$150 million to US$200 million.

Although electricity tariffs are not low by international standards (on average US$4.7 cents/kWh), they are below the level that is necessary to reflect the cost of service and particularly the system expansion. A World Bank study in 2007 revealed that electricity and heat tariffs need to increase by 60 percent to cover costs. Lack of capacity and political will to adjust tariffs in a timely manner, reflecting increasing costs (for fuel, coal, imported spare parts, goods, and equipment) have exacerbated financial losses.

The Energy Regulatory Authority (ERA) of Mongolia also introduced a lifeline tariff rate to mitigate the financial impact on poor and low-income consumers. Though the ERA introduced lifeline tariffs a few years ago, very few households have subscribed for those tariffs largely because of the lack of registration (by newly migrated households) or outstanding payables for previously used electricity. Paying electricity bills is not a problem for most ger area residents, but they would not be able to pay for new connections because most of them are poor. Because of the lack of proper planning and enforcement, it would be problematic to provide new connections, which need to be coordinated with district and city authorities.

The tariff for electricity in ger areas is between 58 and 66 Tg/kWh (US$0.041 and 0.047) without VAT, depending on monthly consumption. Households in ger areas pay around Tg 8,000 to Tg 12,000 per month for electricity; this represents about 4 percent to 5 percent of total income (Tg 200,000 to Tg 250,000, or US$143 to US$179 per month) (see table 8.1).

UBEDN's Performance

UBEDN's overall operational performance has improved considerably over the past three years. Distribution losses (technical and nontechnical) have declined progressively from 28.4 percent in 2005 to 21.7 percent in 2008. The average billing collection rate has been satisfactory and has ranged between 100 percent (in 2007) and 95.9 percent (in 2008). The recent decline in the overall collection rate suggests that older outstanding bills are becoming increasingly more difficult to collect and reflects the current economic downturn.

The underlying growth in demand and reduction in network losses over the past three years has resulted in high sales growth averaging 12.3 percent per year. Total number of customers as of December 31, 2008, reached 176,000, registering an average annual growth of just under 8,200 customers. The average number of customers per employee has gone up marginally from 114 in 2006 to 117 in 2008. The customer mix for 2008 is indicated in table 8.2.

Electricity tariffs increased by 27 percent effective July 15, 2008. The weighted average electricity revenue has increased from 48.51Tg/kWh (US$0.041/kWh) in 2006 to 57.84Tg/kWh (US$0.049/kWh) in 2008, representing growth of 19.2 percent. However, the distribution and supply component of the tariff (that is, excluding bulk supply or power purchase costs) has risen by 40.4 percent from 9.71Tg/kWh (US$0.008/kWh) in 2006 to 13.64Tg/kWh (US$0.049/kWh) in 2008. The following chart illustrates the development of the retail tariff[1] over the past three years.

The overall financial performance of UBEDN has improved over the past three years because of efficiency improvements (lower distribution losses and higher billing collections) and sharp increases in the distribution and supply component (that is, UBEDN's share) of the tariff. The

TABLE 8.1. Electricity Tariffs for Residential Consumers

CUSTOMER GROUPS	TARIFF (Tg/kWh)
UB apartment dwellers	
<150 kWh per month	60.00
151–250 kWh per month	64.00
>251 kWh per month	68.00
UB ger residents	
<150 kWh per month	58.00
151–250 kWh per month	62.00
>251 kWh per month	66.00

Source: UBEDN 2009.

TABLE 8.2. UBEDN Customer Mix

	CUSTOMERS		SALES, GWh	REVENUE, MILLION Tg	AVERAGE TARIFF (Tg/kWh)
Ger area (peri-urban)	92,876	52.8%	222.5 (19.1%)	11,452.9 (17.0%)	51.6
Apartment	73,339	41.7%	167.7 (14.4%)	9,768.6 (14.5%)	58.3
Commercial and industrial (CI)	9,791	5.6%	774.7 (66.5%)	46,081 (68.4%)	59.5
Total	176,006	100%	1,165	67,370	57.8

Source: UBEDN 2009.

collected revenues compared with cash revenue requirements illustrate that the company has closed the financing gap and has lived within its means in the past two years.

UBEDN's distribution and supply costs, other than depreciation, have increased as a percentage of operating revenue from 19.0 percent in 2006 to 19.7 percent in 2008. Payroll costs per employee have risen by 47 percent over the past three years, and total payroll costs accounted for 12.5 percent of operating revenue in 2008. Repairs and maintenance costs in 2008 were 86 percent higher than in 2006 and represented 12.5 percent of operating revenue; however, such costs are still far below system requirements. Depreciation charges are excluded because of a peculiar and unexplained drop, reflected in UBEDN's income statements, from Tg 4.1 billion in 2006 to Tg 1.8 billion in 2008 (US$2.9 million to US$ 1.3 million).

Capital investments during the past three years amounted to US$12.3 million. Of this amount, 49 percent was funded through long-term borrowing and 14 percent through government grants. The remaining 37 percent was financed from UBEDN's internal resources and short-term bank borrowing.

The company's liquidity remains weak, although it has improved since 2006. The current ratio (the proportion of current assets to current liabilities) has gone up from 0.6 in 2006 to 0.8 in 2008. The debt/equity ratio has increased from 98 percent to 103 percent. The unsatisfactorily high ratio is mainly because fixed assets have not been revalued for many years. A professional revaluation of fixed assets is expected to be completed by end 2009.

CURRENT STATUS OF ELECTRICITY IN GER AREAS

Recent household surveys report that more than 95 percent of ger residents in Ulaanbaatar have electricity in their households.[2] Despite the extensive coverage of electricity in the ger areas, the lack of capacity of electricity supply and unreliable service remain as main challenges, often resulting in power outages. The key issues with the electricity supply in ger areas are insufficient capacity of transformers and substations, as well as poor service quality because of the capacity shortage.

Households without access to electricity tend to be those in the fringe ger areas. Though new connections were made in recent years in ger areas, financed from the state and municipal budget, about

TABLE 8.3. Current Status of Electricity Supply in Selected Khoroos

KHOROO	TOTAL HOUSEHOLDS	ELECTRICITY SUPPLY	SERVICE IMPROVEMENTS NEEDED	NO ELECTRICITY
Bayangol district, 11th khoroo	2,970	2,920	30	50
Songino Khairkhan district, 8th khoroo, Bayankhoshuu ger area	1,677	1,677	50	N/A
Bayanzürkh district, 9th khoroo, Sharhad ger area	2,567	2,497	48	70

Source: UBEDN 2009.

8,000 families still do not have electricity in UB. The UBEDN estimated that about Tg 2.8 billion (US$2 million) would be necessary to provide electricity to those households. In the three ger areas under review, only about 120 households are reported to have no access to electricity (table 8.3).

OPTIONS FOR SERVICE IMPROVEMENTS IN GER AREAS

City Center Ger (Naran), 11th Khoroo, Bayangol District

Consumers living in apartments pay slightly higher tariffs than residents in ger areas. The tariff for apartment areas is 68 Tg/kWh, compared to 66 Tg/kWh in ger areas. Connection costs of electricity to residences are presented in the next section.

Midtier Ger Area Bayankhoshuu Ger area, 8th Khoroo, Songino Khairkhan District

This khoroo has eight *khesegs* (microdistricts), six of which have undergone technical rehabilitation under the ESP in 2005–07. This change includes the installation of rubber-insulated aerial conductors (XLPE) cables and electricity tariff meters together with meter boxes. The project implementation in the two remaining khesegs is pending. Within the Ulaabaatar Services Improvement Project (USIP), street lighting has been improved, and 51 lighting fixtures were installed at both ends of eight streets. Cadastre mapping of the khoroo was prepared, including the systematic mapping of hashaas of each kheseg. However, the actual locations of hashaas and streets can be difficult to determine because of poor mapping and labeling in the cadastre system. In general, electricity supply in this khoroo has improved significantly with the implementation of ESP. There are voltage drop issues only on Streets # 8 and # 9 of the Zuun Bayan Tsagaan area for about 40 households; also, some newcomers have not been provided with electricity because of the lack of official registration.

Seven outdoor transformer stations (OTS) and indoor transformer stations (ITS) are in operation in this khoroo, which is located in the *Nuur* (lake) area, where four brick manufacturing factories operate during summer months. Given the high density of the location, it has limited space for newcomers. Sometimes several families live in one hashaa and as a result may easily move to another place without paying their electricity charges. The installation of electricity meters under the technical part of ESP allows the use of time-differentiated meters, while the new XLPE cables help reduce nontechnical losses, such as theft of electricity.

Around 70 households on Eej Khairkhan's 8th Street (or 4th Kheseg) do not have electricity. In addition, around 47 newcomers in the 7th Kheseg settled in a swampy, low-lying area without registering; those households constructed a 0.4kV distribution line privately and have taken electricity only from one pole. In the 6th and 2nd khesegs, 20 households and 30 households, respectively, on 2nd Street are taking electricity from one meter, thus increasing loading and causing voltage drops. Conversely, the central khesegs have a relatively reliable electricity supply where ESP is completed.

In one particular situation, on 8th Street of Eej Khairkhan or Belkh, area households are engaged in cattle breeding; the poor road condition makes the construction of distribution lines very difficult. Generally, the territory of this khoroo has a muddy and craggy surface. Nine OTSs and ITSs are in operation in this khoroo, and the remaining customers are supplied from other OTSs.

Occasional electricity interruptions are reported in this khoroo during evening peak loading. The khoroo is located far from the city center and has a relatively high number of newcomers. Also, temporary households move into the area during the summer season to plant vegetables and to camp, thus increasing electricity demand. It is estimated that annual demand growth will be as much as 5 percent to 6 percent per year. During discussions, khoroo and kheseg leaders noted that the average monthly electricity consumption of ger area households is around 150 kWh or Tg 10,000 without VA.

The western distribution center of UBEDN is responsible for technical aspects of electricity supply, and the Bayangol district customer service center (CSC) is responsible for customer billing and revenue collection, as well as day-to-day service and maintenance.

In the Midtier ger, there is an issue of improving services for about 50 households who live in 8th and 9th Streets of the Zuun Bayan Tsagaan area. The per capita cost of upgrading and rehabilitation is estimated to be about Tg 336,742.6 (about US$230).

Current ger residents will benefit from the improved and reliable supply of electricity, and so the consumption level is likely to rise. Recently, the Project Steering Committee of ESP decided to rehabilitate 38 transformer substations in Songino Khairkhan district at a total cost of around Tg 545.5 million (US$390,000). It is expected that nonrehabilitated khesegs of the 8th khoroo will be included in this work.

Fringe Ger (Sharhad), 9th Khoroo, Bayanzürkh District

Of the eight khesegs in this khoroo, upgrades under the ESP were implemented in six khesegs in 2005–06, including installation of XLPE cables and electricity meters together with meter boxes.

The cost of connections for households without electricity will be around Tg 712,500– Tg 956,783 (US$500–US$670), depending on the distance from existing substations, topography, and so forth (see tables 8.4; 8.5;

TABLE 8.4. Cost of Service Improvements in 8th Khoroo for 50 Households

COST ITEMS	COST (THOUSANDS, TG)
0.4 kV overhead lines, 0.5 km	12,014.6
Meters, boxes, and other	4,822.5
Total	16,837.1

Source: World Bank Task Team estimates 2009.

TABLE 8.5. Cost of New Connections in 9th Khoroo for 60 Households

COST ITEMS	COST (THOUSANDS, TG)
Transformer substation, 160 kVa	18,129.5
10 kV overhead lines, 0.5 km	10,000.1
0.4 kV overhead lines, 1.5 km	21,127.6
Meters, boxes, and other	8,149.8
Total	57,407.1

Source: World Bank Task Team estimates 2009.

TABLE 8.6. Cost of Service Improvements in 9th Khoroo for 48 Households

COST ITEMS	COST (THOUSANDS, TG)
Transformer substation, 100 kVa	15,515.0
10 kV overhead lines, 0.6 km	8,187.8
0.4 kV overhead lines, 0.8 km	16,033.1
Meters, boxes, and other	5,628.3
Total	45,364.3

Source: World Bank Task Team estimates 2009.

and 8.6). The nearby UBEDN network does not have enough capacity, so there is a need to build a new transformer substation with capacity of 160 kVA and an associated distribution network of 10 kV and 0.4 kV overhead lines.

Service improvements for about 48 households in 7th Kheseg of this khoroo would cost about Tg 945,083 (US$660) per household, including a transformer substation of 100 kVa, overhead lines of 10 kV and 0.4 kV, meters, and associated works (see table 8.6).

CONCLUDING REMARKS

There are several major issues with electricity supply in ger areas, including voltage drops caused by capacity shortages, insufficient capacity of transformers and substations, as well as households without electricity. Electricity is provided to most households of the three ger areas under review, except for about 120 newly settled families. ger area residents who have connections on average use about 100 kWh–110 kWh of electricity, for which they pay about 4–5 percent of their monthly income, which is within the internationally recognized affordability limit. Service improvements for existing consumers, such as capacity improvements at nearby substations and improved metering and wiring would cost on average Tg 280,000 to Tg 560,000 (US$200 to US$400) per household.

The cost of new connections for households in the selected ger areas varies between Tg 840,000 and Tg 1,120,000 (US$600 to US$800) per connection depending on (among many variables) topography and distance from and available capacity of nearby transformers and substations of the distribution network. Households currently without connections would not be able to pay for new connections on their own. Even though the Energy Regulatory Authority (ERA) has introduced lifeline tariffs, very few households have subscribed for those tariffs because of a lack of registration (because they are newly migrated), or outstanding payables for previously used electricity. The lack of proper planning and enforcement among district and municipal authorities make it more difficult to provide new connections.

9 Education and Health Services

Social services in education and health are generally in poor condition in ger areas, though they are probably better in terms of access and availability than are most other key infrastructure sectors. Similar to other transition economies, the Mongolian government is traditionally responsible for providing basic health and education services, which are heavily subsidized. In light of a series of policy reforms in recent years, the private sector has played a growing role in those sectors, and the share of private out-of-pocket costs has steadily increased. However, the private cost of schooling and hospitals remains generally low compared with many other transition economies. Despite inefficiencies and structural issues embedded within those sectors, key indicators on educational attainment and health suggest a gradual but steady improvement toward meeting the Millennium Development Goal (MDG) targets.

Improving service delivery in education and health would require addressing a set of related policies, institutional structures, and systems of financial incentives at the national level, which is beyond the scope of this report. This chapter describes some of the relevant sector background, diagnoses key issues in education and health sectors that were highlighted during the focus group discussion in three gers, and summarizes options for service improvements and the financial implications.

CURRENT STATUS OF EDUCATION AND HEALTH SERVICE PROVISION IN GER AREAS

Education. Overall, Mongolia ranks high among countries in the East Asia region in enrollment rates and the percentage of students completing basic education.[1] Nevertheless, enrollment figures mask important disparities in completion rates by geographic area and wealth. Educational attainment in ger areas is lower than that in apartment areas, showing a clear correlation between income and educational levels (figure 9.1). In ger areas, about 37 percent of residents have completed secondary school, 14 percent of children recently have finished primary school, and another 14.5 percent have dropped out of secondary school. In apartment areas, by contrast, almost half of students have advanced past secondary school to vocational training or college education (see figure 9.1).

FIGURE 9.1. Highest Education Level Obtained in Ger and Apartment Areas (%)

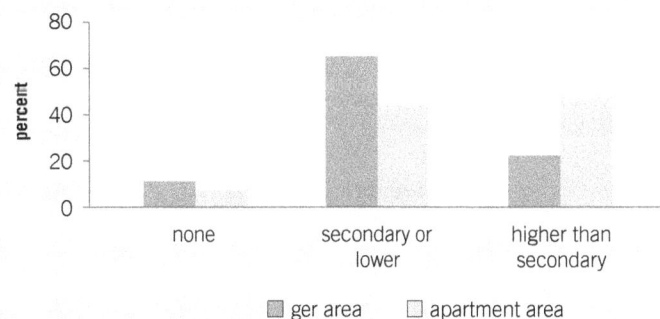

Source: HIES 2007.

The share of government spending devoted to education remains relatively high. Since 1997, when the share of education spending reached a low of 16 percent of the total budget, education's share of the budget has increased,[2] reaching 20 percent of total public expenditures in 2005. This figure is in line with the government's policy to maintain education's share of the total government budget at about 20 percent. This level of spending is relatively high compared to most low-income countries.[3] Total spending on education as a percentage of total public expenditure was 19.1 in 2004 compared with an average of 16.2 percent for other developing countries in East Asia and the Pacific Region.[4]

At the national level, primary and secondary education is given a high priority by the government with the view of achieving the MDG of universal primary education. Strengthening basic education is listed as a priority area in the Government's National Development Strategy Plan.[5] The bulk of funding for pretertiary education continues to come from the state budget. Since 1991, non-state participation in education has increased, and schools have been more active in raising additional sources of revenue. Nevertheless, state financing is by far the largest source of funding for the education sector. Funding through the state budget remains predominant; in 2006, it was estimated at 98 percent. Primary and secondary education receive more than 50 percent of the overall education budget and account for 70 percent of all students in the education system.[6]

The government also runs education aid programs, including tuition subsidies for the poor, plus free textbooks and school supplies. The evaluation of those programs indicates that while there is some leakage to the nonpoor and room for improvement to expand coverage of the poor, the poor do greatly benefit and are the largest share of beneficiaries.

The state financing and aid programs in primary and secondary education translate into relatively low-to-moderate household spending on education. According to the Household Income Expenditure Survey (HIES) analysis, in ger areas, nearly 70 percent of primary and secondary students do not pay any tuition, compared to less than 45 percent in apartment areas (see table 9.1). Among those who do pay for tuition in ger areas for primary and secondary school, the average annual tuition is Tg 50,000 (US$107) per student, compared to Tg 350,000 (US$250) per student in apartment areas. Other than tuition, books, and school supplies, food and transport are the major expenses for primary and secondary education.

Focus group discussions in the three ger areas indicate that the distance and time spent commuting to school do not seem to be much of an issue, although it was often highlighted that students from newly settled, more distant gers would have to walk more than one hour to get to school. About 60–65 percent of primary and secondary students walk to school; the rest rely on public transportation or family

TABLE 9.1. Average Annual Household Expenditure on Primary and Secondary Education (Tg)

AREA	GER AREA	APARTMENT
Rent	169	10,908
Books and supplies	34,893	44,078
Uniforms	11,306	14,957
Transportation	27,178	34,228
Food	29,207	55,611
Others	12,344	22,335
Total	115,098	182,117
% of average income	7.2	7.0
% of students enrolled in public school	89	77
% of HH who pay tuition	30	44

Source: NSO 2008.

vehicles. On average, primary and secondary students are reported to spend about 25–35 minutes getting to school (see table 9.2). This travel time is similar to the result of the HIES survey, which showed average travel times of about 18 minutes for apartment areas and 22 minutes for ger areas.

However, road safety and school transportation are often cited as main areas for improvement in schooling in ger areas. There are virtually no road safety measures in front of or near schools, and this absence increases the incidence of traffic accidents. With almost one-half of the ger students taking some kind of vehicle to go to school, unreliable and infrequent transportation services can add difficulties.

Considering the relatively low drop-out rates, the acceptable educational attainment (by international standards), and the relative affordability per household, the main challenge for primary and secondary schools in ger areas is

TABLE 9.2. Secondary School in Three Ger Areas

	CITY CENTER GER (NARAN)	MIDTIER GER (BAYANKHOSHUU)	FRINGE GER (SHARHAD)
Number of kindergartens	2	1	1
Number of teachers at kindergartens	21	18	18
Enrollment at kindergartens	576	490	190
# of secondary schools	2	1	1
Total number of students in this khoroo enrolled in secondary schools	2,781	500	4,430
Total number of students attending schools	4,580	3,200	1,196
Pupil-teacher ratio (PTR)	N/A	64	35
Number of class shifts per day	3	3 to 4	4
Average travel time (minutes)	25	35	36
Average travel distance	3.2	2.5	1.8

Source: World Bank Task Team Survey 2009 with kheseg leaders during focus group discussion.

to maintain or increase their capacity in response to urban migration and growth. The expansion of ger areas has put significant pressure on existing school facilities. In the three ger areas under review, there are one or two secondary schools with 1,200 to 3,200 students. The pupil-teacher ratio varies from 35:1 to 64:1, compared with 34:1 in Ulaanbaatar (UB) on average. In the Midtier ger, the pupil-teacher ratio is far higher than UB's average mainly because it has to absorb about 2,700 students from neighboring khoroos that do not have a secondary school. Similarly, the City Center ger (Naran) secondary schools accommodate an additional 1,800 students from neighboring khoroos. In the Fringe ger, existing school facilities can serve only 30 percent of the total students in the khoroo. The rest attend schools in neighboring khoroos. All schools run three to four shifts per day to accommodate the growing number of students, appreciably limiting the length of school days for students.

Focus group interviews with khoroo and kheseg leaders show that all schools in ger areas suffer from poor maintenance and a lack of adequate facilities. In case of the Midtier ger, the kindergarten is shared with three neighboring khoroos (No. 17, 19, and 24) and is far too small. Many of those kindergartens are donor funded and rely on external funding for operation and maintenance. If for some reason the budget support or external funding should fall short, most of the facilities will be closed.

The absence of recreational centers for after-school activities is another problem facing ger residents. Schools operate on three or four shifts per day, making after-school activities at school difficult, if not impossible. In all three ger areas, there is no recreational center at the khoroo level. Lack of supervised leisure activities is often cited as a main factor contributing to juvenile crime. When schoolchildren have no constructive way to spend their spare time, they end up wandering in the streets and getting into trouble. In fact, crime in ger areas is emerging as a social issue in UB; this is a common social phenomenon in economies experiencing drastic social and demographic changes, along with rising income inequality. International donors have financed a number of youth centers across ger areas, providing various programs free of charge to children from disadvantaged backgrounds. However, maintenance of the facilities and programs that would continue to attract youth is the main challenge. Such maintenance would require a small but steady and reliable budget allocation from district governments, which are often strapped for cash.

Health Services: Health indicators in Mongolia fare well compared to countries at similar levels of development, reflecting the traditional role of the government as the main provider of health services. Infant and child mortality is low and has been declining steadily. The infant and under-five mortality rates were 35 and 43 per 1,000 in 2007, respectively,[7] and mortality from communicable diseases has also decreased notably, especially for tuberculosis and other diseases that can be prevented with immunization programs.[8] While infant and child mortality seem to be declining, the adult mortality rate is reported to be rising because of lifestyle-related diseases and noncommunicable conditions such as heart attack, stroke, cancer, and diabetes.

The Social Health Insurance introduced in 1994 provides coverage to people in Mongolia. Revenues are based on payroll contributions by individuals in the formal labor market and a flat rate contribution of Tg 500 (US$0.36) by individuals in the informal sector labor market. In addition, full government subsidies apply for vulnerable groups such as the unemployed, children under 16, pensioners, and parents with children under two years old. According to the HIES survey, almost 90 percent of ger residents and slightly less than 95 percent of apartment residents have health insurance. Health care is mainly financed from the government budget. Government expenditures accounted for approximately 63 percent of total health expenditures in 2003. From an international perspective, government spending on health as a share of GPD is high (6.9 percent), and private out-of-pocket expenses are considered low compared with other transition economies.

The government reform in the mid-1990s in the health sector shifted the emphasis of the system from hospitals to a primary health care (PHC) system with support from donors, including the Asian Development Bank and the UN agencies.[9] In line with the government's decentralization policy, responsibility for the health care system was also decentralized to the local governments, who are now mainly responsible for the delivery of health services. Policy making, strategic planning, and evaluation remain as responsibilities of the Ministry of Health (MoH).

In urban areas, PHC services are delivered by family group practices, consisting of community nurses who refer emergency patients to district health centers. Specialized care is delivered by urban district general hospitals, which cover all major clinical specialties and typically have capacities of 200–300 beds for delivering inpatient services.[10] There are also state clinical hospitals and specialized health centers, mainly located in UB city.

One key issue in the health sector is the inefficient allocation of resources between curative hospital services and preventive services. The level of expenditures for hospital care is high—the hospital subsector accounts for about two-thirds of the health budget—compared with the level of spending on public health and primary care.[11] The previously mentioned policy change that emphasizes the PHC system and the decentralization of the responsibilities of the health care system was not accompanied by the sufficient redirection of resources to PHCs and local governments. Consequently, the roles and responsibilities among the MoH and local governments remain unclear. It is often noted that Mongolia has far too many hospitals: 23.4 hospitals per 100,000 people, more than twice the average in the European Union and other transition economies.[12] The hospitals, however, are concentrated in urban areas, and PHCs in remote areas are left without adequate facilities and resources.

Aside from an oversupply of hospital services, the provision of health services in UB is inequitable and favors the nonpoor areas of the city. Despite laws, regulations, and policies that underscore the importance of PHC, financial support for public health has been insufficient. PHC is known to receive only around 5.5 percent of total health funding; the hospital sector, by contrast, continues to account for about two-thirds of the state health budget.

The lack of health care quality and investment in infrastructure, facilities, and equipment are also well illustrated in the three ger areas (table 9.3). PHCs in the ger areas face problems in keeping up with the demand placed on the services. Each khoroo has one or two PHCs, and the ratio of patients to doctors is high compared to a similar PHC in apartment areas. Because of limited budget allocations, the facilities in the areas are reported to have outdated equipment and are understaffed, with fewer than 10 staff per facility, including part-time workers. The health clinics in remote ger areas, in particular, tend to be overcrowded given the lack of alternatives that residents have for primary health providers. In contrast, in the central ger area, the health clinic is usually underutilized as the residents have alternative choices of primary and secondary hospitals, as well as other primary health clinics in the city center.

The focus group discussion highlighted dissatisfaction with the quality and accessibility of primary health services, as well as a lack of trust in primary care providers. Most households would prefer to go to secondary or tertiary level hospitals in the city for better and more reliable services but are often discouraged from doing so because of the much higher cost that individuals have to pay themselves. Although there is no hard data to support this finding in ger areas, community representatives expressed a concern that an increasing number of poor households do not have access to health services because they lack civil registration and are, therefore, not officially entitled to free health and education services or other social welfare benefits, nor are they eligible to register for the social health insurance scheme.

OPTIONS FOR SERVICE IMPROVEMENTS AND FINANCIAL IMPLICATIONS

Improving service delivery in education and health services in ger areas would require a set of policy reforms that revisit the underlying institutional, financing, and incentive systems in the two sectors at the national level. This work goes beyond the scope of the present study. Hence, options discussed here will focus on providing facilities and services in the three ger areas.

TABLE 9.3. Primary Health Providers in Three Ger Areas

	CITY CENTER (NARAN)	MIDTIER GER (BAYANKHOSHUU)	FRINGE GER (SHARHAD)
Population	12,245	7,979	11,130
Number of clinics in khoroo	2	1	1
Number of doctors and nurses in the clinic	6–7	6–7	11
Number of patients received per day	N/A	N/A	240

Source: World Bank Task Team Survey 2009 with kheseg leaders during focus group discussion.

For education:

☐ The most urgent problem in ger area schooling is a lack of facilities to absorb the increasing number of students. This problem can be partly addressed by providing additional primary and secondary schools or expanding the existing ones to ease the burden on existing facilities. Either approach would require not only having physical investments in facilities but also adding teachers and other supporting infrastructure such as roads, water supplies, and sanitation.

☐ An initial assessment suggests costs would be around Tg 1,820,000 (US$1,300) per capita to provide school facilities and supporting infrastructure operating on a normal single shift. This figure does not include costs associated with remuneration for schoolteachers, and so forth. Similarly, the provision of youth and recreational centers should be considered in the ger areas. Around Tg 175,000 (US$125) per capita is estimated for the physical investment only. More important, maintaining existing facilities and programs, which are critical to ensure the long-term sustainability of the centers, will probably add another 10–15 percent to the capital investment cost every year.

☐ In parallel, general improvements in road conditions and connectivity to schools can help improve school access. Increasing the frequency of public buses or minibuses, which students most frequently ride to schools, can be similarly beneficial. Related cost implications are discussed in detail in chapter 5.

For health:

☐ Expanding or adding primary care providers can be especially important in the remote ger areas where the choice of other hospitals is rather limited. This expansion will have to be accompanied by replacing some outdated equipment and ensuring that enough staff members are in place to prevent underuse of the facilities.

☐ An initial cost estimate for additional primary health care facilities suggests around Tg 505,400 (US$361) per capita, not including salaries and other variable costs.

☐ Some health clinics are often underused because of both a shortage of staffing and outdated facilities. This situation is especially common in the ger areas closer to the city center where people have more liberty to choose alternative primary care providers or secondary or tertiary hospitals. In this case, updating existing facilities and adding competent doctors and nurses should be given priority.

10 Conclusion

The following policy directions and scenarios have emerged as a result of the above analyses.

Smart growth: It makes economic sense to adopt "smart growth" policies as the principal directions in the long run, (for example, to increase density in the center of the city where appropriate while controlling further expansion at the outskirts of the city). In general, high density development will make it easier to provide better urban services with higher efficiency and lower cost. The public also has the desire to live in high-density development: low-rise apartments or collective housing with utility services. Realistically, however, the majority of ger areas will remain in their current conditions because achieving higher density development is very complicated, as elaborated below.

Conversion of central gers to apartments will take time: Converting center ger areas into apartment complexes has not progressed as fast as the government had envisaged for several reasons. Most ger area residents cannot afford the cost of apartments in the city center; the lack of mortgage finance also makes buying large assets (such as apartments) difficult for many people; and the absence of a functioning real estate market—including proper methods for determining prices for private land transactions—has impeded the development of new housing.

Retrofitting urban services in midtier gers is exorbitantly expensive: A majority of ger areas outside of the city center are older establishments. Many residents have lived there for a long time and have invested in their dwellings, a large number of which are detached houses. Those residents are relatively content with their neighborhoods and would like to see improved urban services for their houses or development of low-rise, small-scale apartment complexes. The areas are not suitable for conversion to large high-rise apartment complexes—at least for the midterm—mainly because they are not near network infrastructure, except along the major transportation corridors.

Although a minimum level of urban services have reached most of the areas, upgrading services to the full-fledged level now available in apartment areas would be exorbitantly expensive and almost impossible. The unit costs of services to individual houses are several times higher than for apartment units. Instead, improvements in housing—such as conversion to low-rise, smaller collective dwellings, which might make connection to network infrastructure feasible—could be envisaged if residents' income increases. In the meantime, gradually improving services within the affordability limit of residents and public financial resources would seem the most practical approach for the majority of ger areas.

Room for relocating fringe ger residents: The situation in the more remote fringe areas of the city is slightly different. Gers in those areas are inhabited by recent migrants. Their income level is even lower than those of city center residents or the residents of long-established gers. They are farther away from the economic activities of the city and have little access to health and education services. Utility services also are even worse than for residents in established ger areas. Therefore, residents of those fringe gers are very dissatisfied with living conditions and are ready to relocate, if affordable better housing is available elsewhere. But again, affordability is a very serious issue for the residents because of their economic circumstances.

IMPLICATIONS FOR PLANNING AND DEVELOPMENT

Given the previously described situation, seven priority areas require attention by the government:

1. Access roads within ger areas: The majority of the residents in ger areas have lower incomes and are further disadvantaged by very poor access to markets, workplaces, education, and other services. Modest improvements in the secondary access roads from major corridors to inside the khoroos (including basic drainage and street lighting) would give residents major benefits, including easier access by taxis or minibuses and reduced dust, storm water torrents, and crime. Therefore, it would make sense to initiate planning for development of access roads within the khoroos. Community-driven initiatives on land replotting, if appropriate, would also make it easier to plan roads and provide access for utilities.

2. Better heating systems to improve efficiency and reduce air pollution. Because the development of apartment complexes is likely to take a long time, and because most ger areas will not be connected to central heating systems in the near future, short-term measures are needed to improve air quality in the city. Such measures could include better access to cleaner and more efficient stoves and fuels, as well as programs to increase the energy efficiency of houses.

3. Solid waste management and community infrastructure: Solid waste management is often listed by ger area residents as one of their most serious concerns. The current solid waste collection practices seem to be very inefficient and costly. Other community infrastructure and services, such as pathways, footbridges, and community youth centers, also would be helpful in meeting day-to-day needs of many ger area communities, given the lack of proper site development and the shortage of schools and extracurricular activities in ger areas.

4. Research on affordable collective housing in midtier gers: So far, all apartment developments have been concentrated in the center of the city and been targeted only for higher-income residents. Therefore, the development of apartments has not benefited the majority of ger residents. Conversely, some residents in the older, established midtier ger areas located along major roads seem willing to consolidate their individual plots and develop low-rise collective housing, which would provide easier and less costly access to utility services. Therefore, it would make sense to begin reviewing the feasibility of affordable collective housing development along transport corridors and utility supply lines in the established midtier areas.

5. Fringe gers: Providing networked utility services in the fringe ger areas is very expensive. Many residents in those areas are very dissatisfied with current living conditions (including the poor quality and availability of public utility services) and might want to find better housing and economic opportunities elsewhere. For these reasons, a major expansion of networked utilities in the fringe ger areas does not make much economic sense. Instead, services should be provided at the minimum humanitarian level. Since the future of these gers will depend, in part, on the social integration of new migrants, some lessons from social housing in Hong Kong, China, or Singapore might help Mongolia develop clearer policies.

6. *Utility capacity expansion and reforms*: The more residents enjoy a higher standard of living, the higher the required capacity will be for utility services. However, most utility services—water supply, heating, and electricity—already have reached capacity limits. As gradual progress is made on housing and utility services, capacity also can be expanded. Because estimated investment requirements are significant and utility services face considerable financial constraints, pricing reforms, and utility services regulations will be essential prerequisites.

7. *Further research in related sectors*: The municipal budgetary resources of UB are quite limited, at around Tg 30 billion to Tg 60 billion (US\$21 million to US\$43 million) per year. Given the slow implementation of pricing reforms, many infrastructure services in UB already receive large implicit subsidies. Furthermore, expansion of key network infrastructure will easily require investments of Tg 30 billion to Tg 50 billion (US\$21 million to US\$36 million) or more. Other problems noted in this report, including inadequate housing development, lack of mortgage financing, and problems in the banking sector, create additional challenges for the housing sector. Further research on municipal finance and the banking sector, including mortgage financing, might help the government develop clearer policy directions.

Endnotes

Chapter 1

[1] Shlomo et al. 2005.

[2] JICA (Japan International Cooperation Agency) 2008a.

[3] Ibid.

[4] Population of nine districts where majority of ger areas are located. See UB Census 2004.

Chapter 2

[1] Unless otherwise referenced, the data for this chapter were provided by the National Statistical Office's Household Socioeconomic Survey (HIES). For a detailed description of the analysis methodology of the HIES data in this report, see appendix A.

[2] Older than age 16, younger than age 60.

[3] Paid from the Development Fund and contingent on there being money in that fund.

[4] Hodges et al. 2007.

Chapter 3

[1] The total sample size of this survey was 440. The survey was carried out in four areas including three ger areas, plus a representative apartment area with a sample size of 110 in each area. Some results, where appropriate, have been weighted and adjusted to reflect the overall dwelling types (apartment, detached houses, and gers) in the ger areas. The sampling method was based on a random sampling. Given the small sample size, figures and findings here should be taken only as indicative references.

[2] Law on Mongolia Land Fees n.d.

[3] Law on Mongolia Land Fees n.d.

[4] GTZ (Gesellschaft für Technische Zusammenarbeit) 2008.

[5] Generally speaking, the international benchmark for housing affordability is estimated with price to income ratio (PIR). In most countries, an affordable PIR generally ranges from three to five. In the case of Mongolia, this ratio is much higher than the internationally accepted affordability ratio, even in the apartment area.

Chapter 4

[1] COWI 2009.

[2] Ibid.

[3] Centre for Social Development (CSD) in Mongolia 2006a.

[4] COWI 2009, 18.

[5] CSD 2006a.

[6] COWI 2009, 16.

[7] Ibid.

[8] USUG (Water Supply and Sewage Authority Co. of Ulaanbaatar City) 2008.

[9] World Bank team estimate based on USUG 2008 financial statements for the truck department and the piped to kiosk department.

[10] CSD 2006, Table 5.5.

Chapter 5

[1] Present serviceability rating (PSR) is an assessment of pavement serviceability that is based on observation. This subjective scale ranges from 5 (excellent) to 0 (essentially impassable).

[2] JICA (Japan International Cooperation Agency) 2008a.

[3] The Sharhad bus station, which large buses can access, is located in Sharhad Ger, 9th Khoroo, Bayanzürkh District.

[4] Throughout this chapter, figures used for the three khoroos are approximations based on relatively small sample sizes.

[5] Traffic counts, which were taken over a two-day period in April 2009, were observed at Bayangol District, 11th Khoroo, Tasganii Ovoo Intersection; Songino Khairkhan District, 8th Khoroo, Zuunsalaa and Bayankhoshuu Streets; and Bayanzurkh District, 9th Khoroo, National Health Center Intersection.

[6] JICA (Japan International Cooperation Agency) 2008b.

[7] Residents informed the team that the highest number of crimes occurred in areas without lighting.

[8] JICA 2008b.

[9] Ibid.

[10] Estimated costs include all materials, labor, and equipment.

[11] In Mongolia, the cost to construct a 7-m carriageway with 1.5-m shoulders using hot mix pavement is about US$275,000 per km.

[12] Municipal guidelines call for a cement subbase of 20 cm and for two separate applications of asphalt binder material and mineral aggregate on a prepared surface of no more than 1.5 cm each (3 cm total).

[12] This price excludes the cost of simple box culverts (10 m), which range in cost from US$1,500 to US$2,000 each.

[14] Streetlights would be placed every 50 m.

[15] It is assumed that 1-m wide sidewalks and street lighting will be provided on at least one side of all improved roads.

[16] GDP of US$3 billion/50,000 km of network (international, state, and local roads).

[17] Using a rough estimate of 27 km of roads per khoroo, one streetlight every 50 m, and US$1,500 per khoroo per month to maintain street lighting equals US$2.75 per streetlight per month.

Chapter 7

[1] Fuel cost estimates have been done using wholesale prices: 1 ton of coal costs Tg 65,000 (wholesale) and Tg 130,000 (retail); 1 ton of firewood costs Tg 90,000 (wholesale) and Tg 200,000 (retail).

[2] Fuel cost estimates have been done using wholesale prices: 1 ton of coal costs Tg 65,000 (wholesale) and Tg 130,000 (retail); 1 ton of firewood costs Tg 90,000 (wholesale) and Tg 200,000 (retail).

[3] World Bank 2009a.

Chapter 8

[1] For information about HIES (National Statistical Office's Household Socioeconomic Survey), see appendix A.

Chapter 9

[1] World Bank 2008. The completion rate of basic education in Mongolia is 77 percent, which compares with 56 percent in Vietnam, 43 percent in Indonesia, and 38 percent in Cambodia.

[2] Ibid.

[3] Ibid.

[4] Ibid.

[5] ADB (Asian Development Bank) 2008a.

[6] Ibid.

[7] World Bank 2007b.

[8] Ministry of Health, National Center for Health Development n.d.

[9] ADB (Asian Development Bank) 2008b.

[10] Ibid.

[11] World Bank 2008.

[12] ADB 2008b.

Appendixes

APPENDIX A

Technical Note on the Analysis of the 2008 Household Socioeconomic Survey

The detailed data referenced as "HIES" are from the Household Socioeconomic Survey for 2008, conducted by the National Statistical Office of Mongolia. A total of 11,172 households were surveyed, of which 3,571 households are located in Ulaanbaatar (UB). The data set provides information on general socioeconomic characteristics and detailed income and expenditures, including monthly bills for key infrastructure costs. The survey also entails basic access data for electricity, water supply, heating, and consumption. However, it does not include information on quality and reliability of most services, volume of consumption, spatial coordinates, subdistrict (khoroo) identification, or in-depth information for heating, sanitation, and transportation access. In those areas where data were not available in the survey, the chapter was supplemented with data as referenced in footnotes.

Since survey data do not specify individual subdistricts, or khoroos, it was not possible to determine the location of individual households either in ger areas or the apartment-dominated city center. The survey does specify geographic clusters of 10 households,[1] however. So analysts could establish a subsample of households located in ger areas and could compare that to an urban subsample, the dwelling type in each cluster was further analyzed. Because the clusters were not selected on the basis of the type of housing, there are clusters that overlap ger areas and urban apartment areas; in UB, 16 percent of the clusters contain this mix. There was no way of identifying these mixed areas as ger areas or apartment areas; the mixed areas were excluded from the report's subsample. As a result, ger areas as defined by this report contain no apartments, and apartment areas contain no gers or detached houses.

TABLE A.1. A Sample Size Summary for the 2008 Household Socioeconomic Survey

Total sample in Ulaanbaatar (UB)	3,571
- Total households (HHs) living in apartment areas	1,392
- HHs living in gers	819
HHs living in detached houses	1,304
- HHs living in others	20
Total subsample for analysis (% of total UB HHs)	2,978 (83%)
Total HHs surveyed in ger areas	1,808
- HHs living in gers (% of total UB HHs)	693 (20%)
- HHs living in detached houses (% of total UB HHs)	1,103 (31%)
HHs living in apartments (% of total UB HHs)	1,170 (33%)

Source: NSO 2008.

APPENDIX B
City Center Ger Planning Illustrations

FIGURE B.1. Planning Illustrations Including the City Center Ger (Naran), 11th Khoroo, Bayangol District (West)

Source: Municipal Government of Ulaanbaatar City.

FIGURE B.2. Planning Illustrations Including the City Center Ger (Naran), 11th Khoroo, Bayangol District (East)

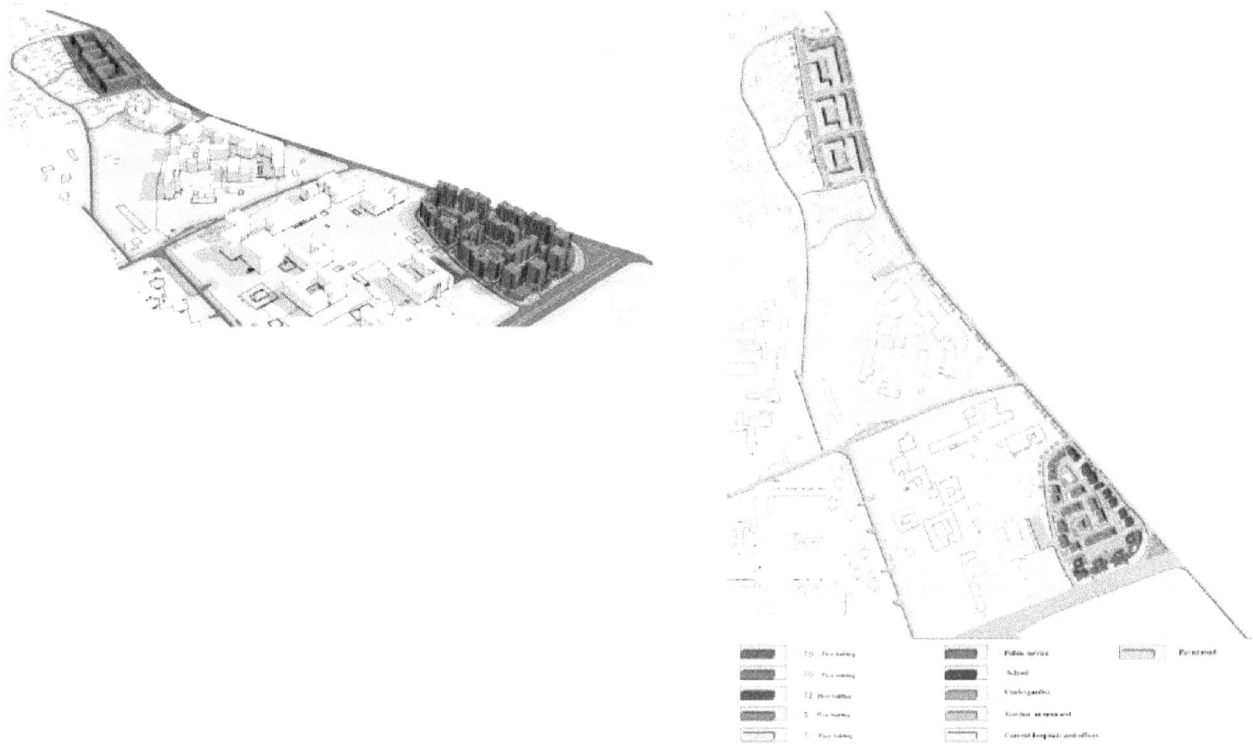

Source: Municipal Government of Ulaanbaatar City.

APPENDIX C
Ulaanbaatar District Statistics

TABLE C.1. Ulaanbaatar District Statistics

							DWELLING TYPE		
#	DISTRICTS	TOTAL AREA (km²)	POPULATION	NUMBER OF KHOROOS	TOTAL FAMILIES	UNEMPLOYMENT (%)	APARTMENTS AND MODERN HOUSES IN HOUSING DISTRICTS	HOUSES IN GER DISTRICTS	GERS
1	Khan-Uul	484.7	94,670	14	23,214	62.4	31,373	40,711	21,586
2	Baganuur	620.2	25,969	4	6,525	55.3	10,424	4,478	10,701
3	Bayanzürkh	1,244.1	221,565	24	51,857	51.7	74,258	75,158	70,347
4	Nalaikh	687.6	28,152	6	7,450	59.1	7,655	13,194	7,127
5	Bayangol	29.5	165,159	20	35,463	53.4	123,778	20,429	20,191
6	Sukhbaatar	208.4	129,486	18	30,137	54.3	58,695	40,338	29,709
7	Chingeltei	89.3	136,014	19	29,270	64	28,827	77,822	28,771
8	Bagahangai	140	3,864	2	876	55	2,062	751	1,034
9	Songinokhairkhan	1,200.6	220,295	25	49,951	57.7	60,323	86,347	73,101
	Ulaanbaatar	**4704.4**	**1,025,174**	**132**	**234,743**	**56.99**	**397,395**	**359,228**	**26,2567**

Source: Municipal Government of Ulaanbaatar City.
Note: Unemployment rate = proportion of the number of unemployed persons, registered in the Department of Labour and Social Welfare, to the economically active population.

APPENDIX D
Distribution and Distances of Water Kiosks

FIGURE D.1. Distance to Nearby Kiosks

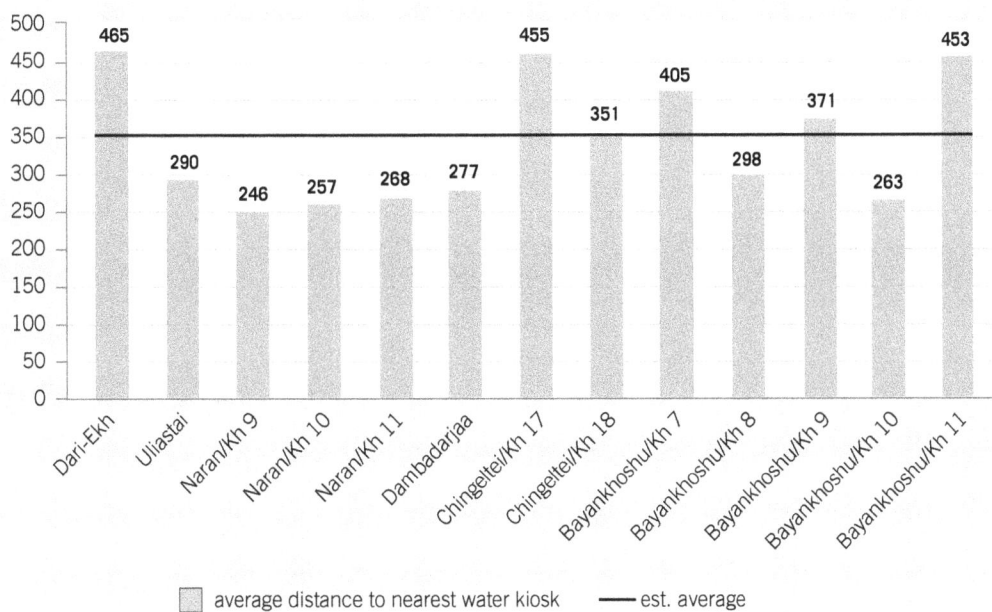

average distance to nearest water kiosk — est. average

Source: Ulaanbaatar Municipal Government Center for Social Development 2006.

TABLE D.1. Distribution of Kiosks in Ger Areas of UB

DISTRICT	TOTAL POPULATION	GER AREA	TOTAL NUMBER OF KIOSKS	TRUCK-SUPPLIED USUG KIOSKS	PIPE-SUPPLIED USUG KIOSKS	PRIVATE KIOSKS	RED CROSS KIOSKS	SPRINGS
Khan Uul	59,088		53	10	37	3	3	—
	12,611	Nisekh		2	16	—	—	—
	23,322	Yarmaq		1	18	—	1	—
	1,909	Blokombinat		3	—	—	1	—
	116	Devshi SAA		1	—	1	—	—
	3,552	Taini		2	—	—	1	—
	3,006	Tuul Tosgon		1	—	2	1	—
		Sonsgolon		—	1	—	—	5
Bayanzürkh	137,431		152	84	22	34	7	—
	9,076	Amagalan		8	1	12	—	—
	5,185	Attan-Ulgil		9	—	1	1	—
	9,576	Dar-Ekn		17	—	5	3	2
	30,391	Shar Khad		8	17	1	1	1
	5,493	Tsaiz		9	—	—	1	—
	15,785	Ulastal		13	1	10	1	1
	2,804	Knonkhor		5	—	3	—	1
	6,389	Ulaan-Khuaran		7	—	—	1	1
	6,884	Tsagaan-Khuaran		4	1	—	—	—
	7,840	Naran-Tuul		4	2	2	—	—
	6,600	Kino-Ulidver		—	2	—	—	—
Bayangol	40,688		44	35	6	3	—	—
	6,830	Gandan		—	6	—	—	—
	11,526	Naran		15	—	—	—	—
	10,274	Shine-Gemtel		9	—	2	—	—
	10,547	Lrhorpoloinar		8	—	1	—	—
Sukhbaatar	65,530		46	39	—	7	—	—
	17,236	Dambadarjaa		9	2	3	—	—
	9,290	Belkhi		5	—	4	—	—
	4,052	Salkhit		3	1	—	—	—

		Population						
Chingeltel	Dolocn Buudai	1,679		8	—	—	—	—
	Guch nkhoyor	13,156		7	—	—	—	—
	Nogoonnuur	7,725		3	3	—	—	0
	Chingeltel	103,572	123	44	66	11	2	—
	Chingeltel	23,783		23	1	4	—	—
	Denjiln Myanga	25,327		4	22	2	2	—
	Khallaast	39,152		8	43	3	—	—
	Zuragt	1,083		9	—	1	—	—
Songino Khairkhan		149,294	143	91	21	26	3	2
	Bayanhoshuu	53,149		56	1	14	1	—
	Tolgoit	44,283		23	23	6	—	—
	Zuunsalaa	2,745		3	—	4	—	—
	Zeel	635		2	—	2	1	—
	Khaniin	7,243		5	—	—	—	—
Total		**555,603**	**561**	**297**	**161**	**84**	**14**	**5**

Source: Ulaanbaatar Municipal Government.
Note: — = 0 (no kiosk).

APPENDIX E
Plan of Water Supply Pilot Project in Dambadarjaa

FIGURE E.1. Plan of Water Supply Pilot Project in Dambadarjaa

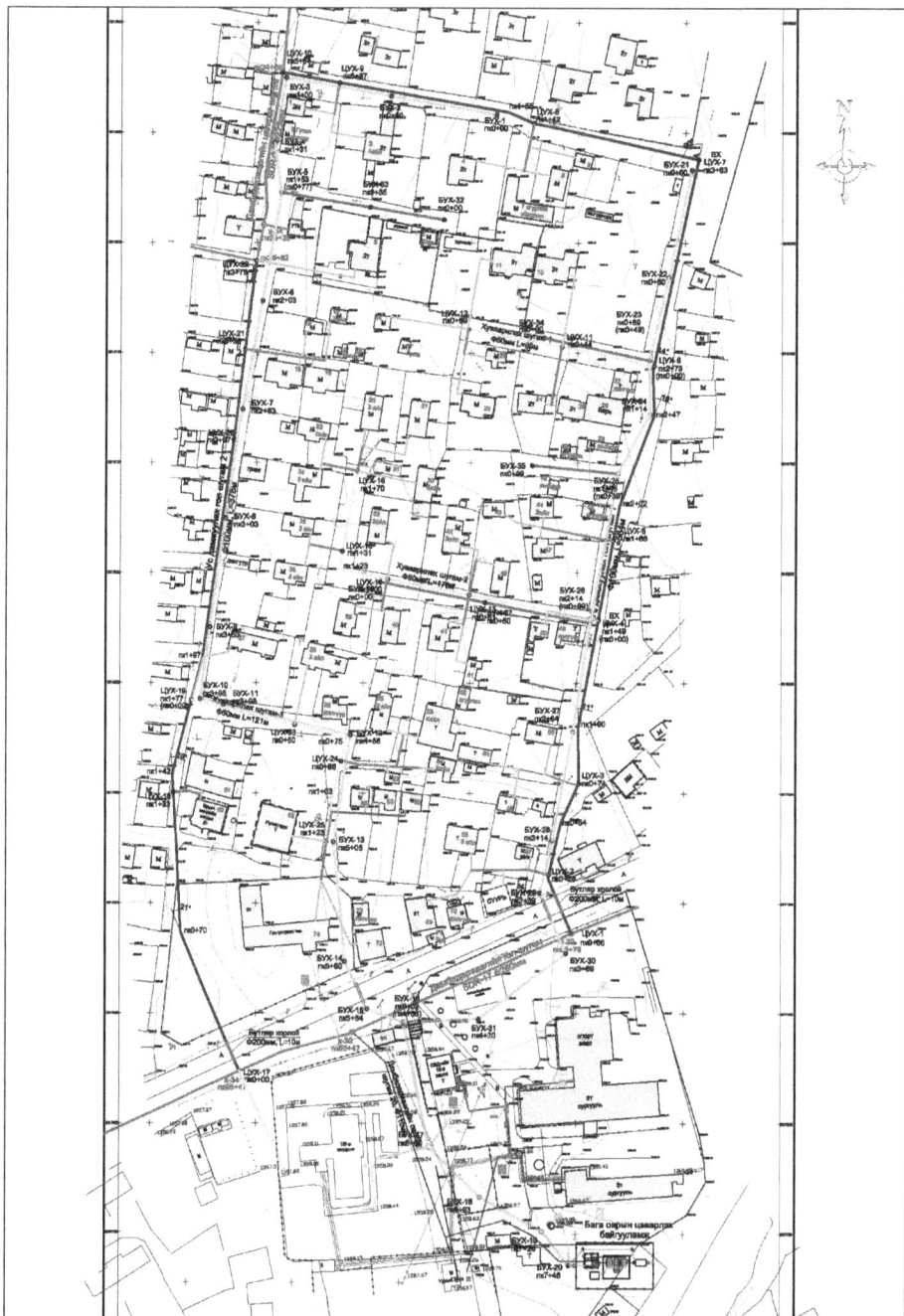

Source: USIP2 PMU.

References

ADB (Asian Development Bank). 2008a. "Mongolia: Education Sector Reform." Technical Assistance Report, ADB, Manila, Philippines.

———. 2008b. "Evaluation on the Health and Social Protection in Mongolia." ADB, Manila, Philippines.

———. 2005. "Mongolia: Urban Development and Housing Sector Strategy." ADB, Manila, Philippines.

Centre for Social Development (CSD) in Mongolia. 2006a. "The Current Situation of the Public Utility Services of the Ger Areas in Ulaanbaatar." Study Report, CSD, Ulaanbaaatar, Mongolia.

———. 2006b. "Community-Service Social Development Project." CSD, Ulaanbaatar, Mongolia.

COWI. 2009. "Mongolia: Exploring Options for Management Contracting-Out in Water Supply and Sanitation Services for Ger Areas in Ulaanbaatar: Progress Report A." World Bank/PPIAF, Washington, DC, March.

GTZ (Gesellschaft für Technische Zusammenarbeit). 2008. "Land Management—Fiscal Cadastre in Mongolia." GTZ, Erschborn, Germany, April.

Energy Research and Development Center. 2002. "Capacity Building in Energy Planning." Energy Research and Development Center, Ulaanbaatar, Mongolia.

HIES (Household Socioeconomic Survey). n.d. Ulaanbaatar, Mongolia.

Hodges, Anthony, et al. 2007. "Child Benefits and Poverty Reduction: Evidence from Mongolia's Child Money Programme." Working Paper, UNICEF, New York, May. www.unicef.org/videoaudio/PDFs/Child_Benefits_and_Poverty_Reduction_Evidence_from_Mongolia.pdf.

JICA (Japan International Cooperation Agency). 2008a. "The Study on City Master Plan and Urban Development Program of Ulaanbaatar City." Working Paper, JICA, Toyko, Japan, July.

———. 2008b. "Databook on Socio-Economic and Environmental Conditions of Ulaanbaatar City." JICA, Tokyo, Japan, May.

Law on Mongolia Land Fees, Article 3. n.d. Government of Mongolia, Ulaanbaatar.

Ministry of Health, National Center for Health Development. n.d. "Health Indicators of 2004." Government of Mongolia, Ulaanbaatar.

National Statistical Office. 2008. "Household Socioeconomic Survey." National Statistical Office, Ulaanbaatar, Mongolia.

Shlomo, Angel, et al. 2005. "The Dynamics of Global Urban Expansion." Transport and Urban Development Department, World Bank, Washington, DC, September.

Ulaanbaatar Census. 2004. The Municipal Government of Ulaanbaatar City, Mongolia.

UNICEF (United Nations Children's Fund). 2007. "Child Benefit and Poverty Reduction: Evidence from Mongolia's Child Money Program." UNICEF, New York.

USAID (United States Agency for International Development). 2007. "A Review of the Mongolian Primary Mortgage Market." USAID, Washington, DC.

USUG (Water Supply and Sewage Authority Co. of Ulaanbaatar City). 2008. Financial and management performance data.

World Bank. 2009a. "Energy Efficient and Cleaner Heating in Poor, Peri-Urban Areas of Ulaanbaatar, Summary Report on Activities." World Bank, Washington, DC.

———. 2009b. "Task Team Survey 2009." World Bank, Washington, DC.

———. 2008. *Mongolia: Consolidating the Gains, Managing Booms and Busts, and Moving to Better Service Delivery, A Public Expenditure and Financial Management Review.* Washington, DC: World Bank.

———. 2007a. "Rethinking the Delivery of Infrastructure Services in Mongolia." World Bank, Washington, DC.

———. 2007b. "World Development Indicators." 2007. World Bank, Washington, DC.

———. 2006a. "Hygiene and Sanitation Situation Report for Ger Areas, Mongolia." World Bank, Washington, DC.

———. 2006b. "Mongolia: Human Development Sector Report." World Bank, Washington, DC.

World Bank and PPIAF (Public-Private Infrastructure Advisory Facility). 2009. *Southern Mongolia Infrastructure Strategy.* Washington, DC: World Bank and PPIAF.

Index

Boxes, figures, maps, notes, photos, and tables are indicated by *b, f, m, n, p,* and *t,* respectively.

A

Administration of Land Affairs, Geodesy, and Cartography (ALAGaC), 15
Asian Development Bank (ADB), 8

B

bathhouses, 61, 62, 66, 67
Bayankhoshuu, as proxy midtier ger, xvi, 3, 10, 10*p,* 13*m. See also* midtier gers
benefits, governmental, 8, 8*f*
boilers. *See* heat-only boilers (HOBs) and coal-fired water heaters

C

Cambodia, 86*n*1
central energy system (CES), 59, 60
central gers. *See* city center gers
centralized heating. *See* district or centralized heating
CES (central energy system), 59, 60
Child Money Program (CMP), 8
CHP (combined heat and power) production, 59, 60
city center gers
    current status and development assumptions, 9, 9*p,* 12*m*
    education and health care
        number of health providers and patients, 79*t*
        number of schools and students, 77*t*
    electricity in, 72, 72*t*
    heating
        current systems, 60–61, 61*t*
        service improvement options and costs, 62–63, 63*t,* 67
    income levels in, 17
    land and housing
        household preferences
            for dwelling type and development pattern, 21–22, 21*t,* 22*t*
        owning versus renting, 18*t*
        policy directions, xx, 23–24, 23*t,* 81
        prices and financing, 19, 19*t,* 20*t*
        satisfaction with, 20–21, 20*t,* 21*t*
        size of, 18*t*
        types of housing, 17, 18*t*
    Naran as proxy ger for, xvi, 3, 9, 9*p,* 12*m*
    planning illustrations, 9, 92–93*f*
    roads and public transportation in
        current state of public transportation, 35, 36*t,* 39*p*
        current state of roads, 34, 34*t,* 38*p*
        service improvements, 37–40, 40*t*
    solid waste management in
        collection of garbage, 46, 47*f,* 47*t,* 48*t*
        financial service improvement implications, 48, 49*t,* 53, 54
        service improvement options for, 48, 49*f,* 49*t*
        tariff structure, 48, 48*t*
    water supply and sewerage, 25*t,* 27–29, 27*t*
CMP (Child Money Program), 8
coal-fired water heaters. *See* heat-only boilers (HOBs) and coal-fired water heaters
combined heat and power (CHP) production, 59, 60
community infrastructure, need for, xxi, 82

Compact City concept, vii, xv, 1–2
cost-benefit analyses for different development
     paths, xv–xx, 2, 3
currency equivalents, xi

D
Dambadarjaa water supply pilot project, 30*f*,
     98*f*
demographics
     of ger areas, 6, 6*t*
     household, 16–17, 16*t*
district or centralized heating, 59–60
     in city center gers, 62–63, 63*t*
     financial viability of, 67, 68
     in midtier gers, 65–66, 66*t*
district statistics, UB, 94*t*
drinking water. *See* water supply and sewerage
düüregs, xi, 5, 5*t*

E
economic activities in ger areas, 6–7, 7*f*
education and health care, xix–xx, 75–80. *See
     also under* specific ger areas
     basic education completion rates, 86*n*1
     current status of, 75–79, 75*f*, 76*t*, 77*t*,
          79*t*
     ger versus apartment areas, education in,
          75, 75*f*
     recreational facilities and programs, 77–78
     service improvement options and costs,
          79–80
electricity, xix, 69–74
     CHP production, 59, 60
     in city center gers, 72, 72*t*
     conclusions regarding, 74
     current system, 69–72, 70–72*t*
     heating and, 59–60
     in midtier gers, 72–73, 73*t*
     service improvement options and costs,
          72–74, 73–74*t*
     tariffs, 69, 70*t*
     UBEDN, 69, 70–71, 71*t*, 72, 74
employment statistics, 6–8, 7*f*, 8*f*, 16–17, 17*t*
Energy Regulatory Authority (ERA) of
     Mongolia, 70, 74
energy use. *See* electricity; heating

environmental issues
     heating systems, xxi, 59, 82
     landfills, 45–46, 54–55
     limited basic services in ger areas, xv, 1
     pit latrines, 27
     recycling, 46
     satisfaction of residents with living
          environment, 20–21, 21*t*
     zoning, 15
ERA (Energy Regulatory Authority) of
     Mongolia, 70, 74

F
fringe gers
     current status and development
          assumptions, 10, 10*p*, 14*m*
     education and health care
          number of health providers and
               patients, 79*t*
          number of schools and students, 77*t*
     electricity in, 71, 72, 72*t*, 73–74, 74*t*
     heating
          current systems, 61*t*, 62
          service improvement options and
               costs, 66–67, 67*t*, 68*t*
     land and housing
          household preferences
               for dwelling type and
                    development pattern, 21–22,
                    21*t*, 22*t*
          ownership versus rental, 18–19, 18*t*
          policy directions, xx–xxi, 24, 24*t*,
               81–82
          prices and financing, 19, 19*t*, 20*t*
          satisfaction with, 20–21, 20*t*, 21*t*
          size of land plots, 18, 18*t*
          types of housing, 17, 18*t*
     networked utility services for, xxi–xxii,
          82–83
     roads and public transportation in
          current status of public
               transportation, 35, 36*t*
          current status of roads, 34*t*, 43*p*
          service improvements, 42–44, 44*t*
     Sharhad as proxy ger for, xvi, 3, 10, 10*p*,
          14*m*

solid waste management in
        collection of garbage, 46, 47f, 47t,
            48t
        financial service improvement
            implications, 51t, 52t, 53–55,
            54t
        service improvement options for,
            50–53, 51t, 52f, 52t, 53f, 54t, 55t
        tariff structure, 48, 48t
    unemployment and income levels in, 17
    water supply and sewerage, 25t, 27t,
        31–32, 31t, 32t

G

garbage. *See* solid waste management
GDP. *See* gross domestic product
ger areas, 5–14. *See also* city center gers; fringe
    gers; midtier gers
        access roads within, xxi, 82
        community infrastructure, need for, xxi,
            82
        defined, vii, ix, 2b, 2p
        education in ger versus apartment areas,
            75, 75f
        expansion of, xv, 1
        government and administrative
            structure, 5–6, 5t
        limited basic services in, xv, 1
        proxies for different development paths,
            xvi, 3
        socioeconomic structure, 6–8, 6t, 7f, 8f
        Ulaanbaatar (UB), map of 11m
gers, ix, 2b, 2p, 17
government benefits, 8, 8f
gross domestic product (GDP)
        road maintenance costs as percentage
            of, 37
        Ulaanbaatar (UB) generating more than
            60 percent of, xv, 1

H

hashaas, xi, xvi, 18, 18t
health care. *See* education and health care
heat-only boilers (HOBs) and coal-fired water
    heaters, 59, 60
        financial viability of, 67, 68

        in fringe gers, 66–67, 67t, 68t
        in midtier gers, 63–65, 64t, 65t
heating, xviii–xix, 59–68. *See also under* specific
    ger areas
        bathhouses, 61, 62, 66, 67
        conclusions regarding, 67–68
        current systems, 59–62, 61t
        district or centralized heating. *See*
            district or centralized heating
        electricity and, 59–60
        environmental issues, xxi, 59, 82
        as financial burden, 68
        insulation, 60, 65, 67
        policy directions for, xxi, 82
        service improvement options and costs,
            62–68, 63–68t
heating stoves, 59, 60, 67, 68
HIES (Household Socioeconomic Survey), 6,
    16, 76, 77, 78, 91, 91t
HOBs. *See* heat-only boilers (HOBs) and
    coal-fired water heaters
Hong Kong, China, xxii, 83
Household Socioeconomic Survey (HIES), 6,
    16, 76, 77, 78, 91, 91t
housing. *See* land and housing

I

IMF (International Monetary Fund), 8
income in ger areas, 7–8, 7f, 8f, 17, 17t
Indonesia, 86n1
insulation, 60, 65, 67
International Monetary Fund (IMF), 8

J

Japan, 1, 8

K

khesegs, xii, 5, 5t
khoroos
        defined, xii
        dwelling type and development pattern
            preferences in, 21–22, 21t, 22t
        in government and administrative
            structure, 5–6, 5t
        proxy ger areas based on, xvi, 3
        as unit of analysis, 4

kiosks supplying public water, 25–27, 25p, 25t, 28p, 95–97t

L

land and housing, xvi, 15–24. *See also* specific ger areas
   demographics, household, 16–17, 16t
   dwelling type and development pattern preferences, 21–22, 21t, 22t, 23
   government administration of, 15–16
   hashaas, xi, xvi, 18, 18t
   laws, registration procedures, and land fees, 2, 15, 16
   ownership versus rental, 18–19, 18t
   policy directions, xx, xxi, 22–24, 23t, 81–82
   prices and financing, 19, 19t, 20t, 85n5
   satisfaction with, 20–21, 20t, 21t
   size of, 18, 18t
   survey sample size for, 85n1
   types of housing, 17, 18t
   zoning, 15
landfills, 45–46, 54–55
lighting. *See* electricity

M

MDG-based Comprehensive National Development Strategy (2007), 1
medical care. *See* education and health care
midtier gers
   Bayankhoshuu as proxy ger for, xvi, 3, 10, 10p, 13m
   current status and development assumptions, 10, 10p, 13m
   education and health care
      inadequacy of school facilities, 77
      number of health providers and patients, 79t
      number of schools and students, 77t
   electricity in, 72–73, 73t
   heating
      current systems, 61–62, 61t
      service improvement options and costs, 63–66, 64–66t, 67
   land and housing

      affordable low-rise collective housing, development of, xxi
      household preferences
         for dwelling type and development pattern, 21–22, 21t, 22t
      owning versus renting, 18t
      policy directions, xx, 24, 24t, 81, 82
      prices and financing, 19t, 20t
      satisfaction with, 20–21, 20t, 21t
      size of, 18t
      types of housing, 17, 18t
   roads and public transportation in
      current status of public transportation, 35, 36t
      current status of roads, 33p, 34t
      service improvements, 41–42, 42t
   solid waste management in
      collection of garbage, 46, 47f, 47t, 48t
      financial service improvement implications, 51t, 52t, 53–55, 54t
      service improvement options for, 50–53, 51t, 52f, 52t, 53f, 54t, 55t
      tariff structure, 48, 48t
   unemployment and income levels in, 17
   water supply and sewerage, 25t, 27t, 29–31, 30f
migration to UB, xv, 1, 2
Mongolia, urban planning in. *See* urban planning in Mongolia
municipal roads. *See* roads and public transportation

N

Naran, as proxy city center ger, xvi, 3, 9, 9p, 12m. *See also* city center gers
National Land Information System, 16

P

pensions, state, 8
PHC (primary health care) system, 78–79
pit latrines, 27

policy directions, xx–xxii, 81–83
    cost-benefit analyses of different
        development paths, xv–xvi, 2, 3
    current plans, 1–2
    further research, need for, xxii
    heating, xxi, 82
    in land and housing, xx, xxi, 22–24, 23t,
        81–82
    networked utility services for fringe
        gers, xxi–xxii, 82–83
    report aimed at suggesting, vii
    roads and public transportation, xxi, 82
    solid waste management, xxi, 82
    utility capacity expansion and reform,
        xxii, 83
power. See electricity
present serviceability rating (PSR), 34, 86n1
primary health care (PHC) system, 78–79
PSR (present serviceability rating), 34, 86n1
public transportation. See roads and public
    transportation
public water kiosks, 25–27, 25p, 25t, 28p,
    95–97t

R
real estate. See land and housing
recreational facilities and programs, 77–78
recycling, 46
refuse. See solid waste management
retirement benefits, state, 8
roads and public transportation, xvii, 33–44.
    See also under specific ger areas
    access roads within ger areas, xxi, 82
    current status
        of public transportation, 34–35,
            35t, 36t
        of roads, 33–34, 33p, 34t
    policy directions for, xxi, 82
    schools, access to, 80
    service improvements for
        challenges, 36–37
        city center gers, 37–40, 40t
        construction and maintenance
            costs, 37, 39–42, 40t, 42t, 44,
            44t
        fringe gers, 42–44, 44t

midtier gers, 41–42, 42t
    options, 36
traffic counts, 35, 36t, 86n5

S
sanitation. See water supply and sewerage
schools. See education and health care
settlement fees, attempt to impose, 2
sewers. See water supply and sewerage
Sharhad, as proxy fringe ger, xvi, 3, 10, 10p,
    14m. See also fringe gers
Singapore, xxii, 83
smart growth policies, xx, 81
Social Health Insurance, 78
social services. See education and health care
socioeconomic structure of ger areas, 6–8, 6t,
    7f, 8f
solid waste management, xviii, 45–57. See also
    under specific ger areas
    collection of garbage, 46–48, 47f, 47t,
        48t
    current system, 45–48, 45f, 47f, 47t,
        48t
    landfills, 45–46, 54–55
    policy directions for, xxi, 82
    recycling, 46
    service improvements
        city center gers, options for, 48,
            49f, 49t
        financial and economic
            implications of, 53–55, 56t,
            57t
        midtier and fringe gers, options
            for, 50–53, 51t, 52f, 52t, 53f,
            54t, 55t
        residents, collection by, 50, 52f,
            52t, 53–54, 66t
        sanitation workers, collection by,
            50, 51t, 53, 54, 55t
        tariff structure, 55, 55t, 57t
        trash chutes, 48, 49f
        vehicle-based collection, 48, 49t,
            51–53, 53f, 54, 54t, 55t
    tariff structure, 48, 48t, 55, 55t, 57t
    zud affecting, 46, 48

T

traffic counts, 35, 36t, 86n5

transportation. *See* roads and public
transportation

trash. *See* solid waste management

U

UB City Urban Development Master Plan
(2008), vii, xv, 1

UBEDN (Ulaanbaatar Electricity Distribution
Network Company), 69, 70–71, 71t, 72, 74

Ulaanbaatar (UB), urban planning for. *See*
urban planning in Mongolia

Ulaanbaatar Electricity Distribution Network
Company (UBEDN), 69, 70–71, 71t, 72, 74

unemployment, 6–8, 7f, 8f, 16–17, 17t

urban planning in Mongolia, xv–xxii, 1–4
cost-benefit analyses for different
development paths, xv–xvi, 2, 3
definitions pertinent to, xi–xiii
district statistics, UB, 94t
electricity, xix, 69–74. *See also* electricity
further research, need for, xxii
ger areas, 5–14. *See also* ger areas
heating, xviii–xix, 59–68. *See also*
heating
land and housing, xvi, 15–24. *See also*
land and housing
map of UB, 11m
methodology and scope of report, 3–4
migration to UB, xv, 1, 2
policy directions for, xx–xxii, 81–83. *See*
also policy directions
roads and public transportation, xvii,
33–44. *See also* roads and public
transportation
social services, xix–xx, 75–80. *See also*
education and health care
solid waste management, xviii, 45–57.
See also solid waste management
water supply and sewerage, xvi–xvii,
25–32. *See also* water supply and
sewerage

USUG (Water Supply and Sewage Authority
Company of UB City), 25, 26–27, 30, 32

utilities. *See also* electricity; heating; water
supply and sewerage
capacity expansion and reform, xxii, 83
fringe gers, networked utility services
for, xxi–xxii, 82–83

V

Vietnam, 86n1

W

waste. *See* solid waste management; water
supply and sewerage

Water Supply and Sewage Authority Company
of UB City (USUG), 25, 26–27, 30, 32

water supply and sewerage, xvi–xvii, 25–32
additional water sources, 29
bathhouses, 61, 62, 66, 67
city center gers, 25t, 27–29, 27t
costs, 26, 26t
city center gers, 27–28
fringe gers, 31–32, 31t, 32t
midtier gers, 29–30, 30f
Dambadarjaa water supply pilot project,
30f, 98f
fringe gers, 25t, 27t, 31–32, 31t, 32t
midtier gers, 25t, 27t, 29–31, 30f
pit latrines, 27, 27t
public water kiosks, 25–27, 25p, 25t,
28p, 95–97t
service improvement options and costs,
28–29, 30–31, 32
transportation of water to housing, 26, 26p
wastewater
disposal of, 27
treatment plant, 29

World Bank, 8, 69

Z

zoning, 15

zud
defined, xiii
migration due to, xv, 1
solid waste quantities and tariffs during,
46, 48

Eco-Audit

Environmental Benefits Statement

The World Bank is committed to preserving endangered forests and natural resources. The Office of the Publisher follows the recommended standards for paper usage set by the Green Press Initiative, a nonprofit program supporting publishers in using fiber that is not from endangered forests.

In the printing of *Managing Urban Expansion in Mongolia: Best Practices in Scenario-Based Urban Planning*, we took the following measures to reduce our carbon footprint:

- ☐ We used paper containing 50 percent recycled fiber made from post-consumer waste; each pound of postconsumer recycled fiber that replaces a ton of virgin fiber prevents the release of 2,108 pounds of greenhouse gas emissions and lessens the burden on landfills.
- ☐ We used paper that is chlorine-free and acid-free.
- ☐ We printed with vegetable-based inks made from renewable sources and easier to remove in the recycling process.

These measures in printing *Managing Urban Expansion in Mongolia: Best Practices in Scenario-Based Urban Planning* **saved the following:**

We saved:

- ☐ 6 trees
- ☐ 2 million BTUs of total
- ☐ 553 lbs. of net greenhouse gases
- ☐ 2,666 gallons of waste water
- ☐ 162 lbs. of solid waste